I Am the Gate

The Meaning of Initiation and Discipleship

*the text of this book is printed
on 100% recycled paper*

I Am the Gate

The Meaning of Initiation and Discipleship

by

Bhagwan Shree Rajneesh

edited by ma satya bharti

HARPER COLOPHON BOOKS
Harper & Row, Publishers
New York, Hagerstown, San Francisco, London

I AM THE GATE. Copyright © 1975, 1977 by Rajneesh Foundation. All rights reserved. Printed in the United States of America. No part of this book may be used or reproduced in any manner without written permission except in the case of brief quotations embodied in critical articles and reviews. For information address Harper & Row, Publishers, Inc., 10 East 53d Street, New York, N. Y. 10022. Published simultaneously in Canada by Fitzhenry & Whiteside Limited, Toronto.

Designed by Eve Callahan

First U.S. edition: HARPER COLOPHON BOOKS, 1977

LIBRARY OF CONGRESS CATALOG CARD NUMBER: 76–51584

INTERNATIONAL STANDARD BOOK NUMBER: 0–06–090573–5

77 78 79 80 81 82 5 4 3 2 1

CONTENTS

Books by Bhagwan Shree Rajneesh
A Partial List

The Ultimate Alchemy. 2 vols.
(On the Atma Puja Upanishad)

The Book of the Secrets. 5 vols.*
(On tantra)

*Yoga: The Alpha and the
Omega.* 5 vols.
(On Patanjali's yoga sutras)

Roots and Wings
(On Zen)

No Water, No Moon
(On Zen)

The Mustard Seed
(On The Gospel according to
Thomas)

Neither This nor That
(On Tao)

. . . And the Flowers Showered
(On Zen)

Returning to the Source
(On Zen)

The Hidden Harmony
(On the Fragments of
Heraclitus)

Only One Sky
(On Tibetan tantra)

Just Like That
(On Sufism)

Tao: The Three Treasures
4 vols.
(On Lao Tzu)

Meditation: The Art of Ecstasy†
(On techniques of meditation)

Hammer on the Rock
(Meetings with the Master)

When the Shoe Fits
(On Chuang Tzu)

The Empty Boat
(On Chuang Tzu)

Come Follow Me. 4 vols.
(On Jesus)

The True Sage
(On Hasidism)

Until You Die
(On Sufism)

*My Way: The Way of the
White Cloud*
(Questions and answers)

Dimensions beyond the Known
(An autobiography)

*vol 1 published by Harper & Row
†published by Harper & Row

Introduction

I loved the first book I ever read by Bhagwan Shree Rajneesh so much that I could scarcely read it. I read a phrase, a sentence, and got up and danced. I couldn't believe it. Here in Bhagwan Shree's words was everything I had ever believed, everything I had ever suspected, all articulated so lucidly, so poetically, that all I could say was, "Yes!" Yes and thank you. A thousand thanks.

It was the beginning of an intense romance, one that has grown deeper with the years. The relationship between master and disciple, Bhagwan Shree explains, is a relationship of deep love, deep trust. Upon my first reading of that first pamphlet five years ago, the foundation of a growing love developed and before long, despite myself, despite my predilection to reject religion, to be disinterested in meditation, to be skeptical, indeed mocking, of the whole "guru trip," I became a disciple of Bhagwan Shree's. The initiation was a technique, as the meditation methods he devises are techniques, as his words are techniques, as this book itself is a technique. Bhagwan Shree uses everything to take us from where we are to where we can be. He tricks us, he lures us, he seduces us into transformation. And he does it with so much warmth, with so much love, that even in the midst of the inevitable discomfort that accompanies growth, all one can say is, "Yes. And thank you. A thousand thanks."

In the discourses contained in this volume, given in the spring of 1971, Bhagwan Shree talks extensively about how he works with his disciples. Not only does he talk about the techniques he uses, and the esoteric meaning behind them, but he uses his very words as a technique to push one beyond mind, beyond intellect. "Only if you become convinced that what I have said is rational," he explains, "can I begin to work with the irrational. That is the real beginning, but I will have to come to your heart by and by, I will have to go around and around, through your intellectual bypasses."

He begins with the intellect in order to take one beyond intellect. Just when one is convinced by his words, he uses his words to shatter one's convictions. He tells us that Buddha used to tell his disciple Sariputra absurd things just to see whether Sariputra would question him, just to test Sariputra's surrender. Bhagwan Shree seems to do the same. If you are a follower of Buddha or Christ or Gurdjieff or Krishnamurti, Bhagwan Shree will say things that are absolutely unacceptable. If you are a Jew, he will say things about Hitler that are impossible to accept. All of it is a technique, all of it is to create a situation where you are forced to confront your own prejudices, your own blindnesses, your own projections.

If a master gives you something that the human mind will ordinarily question and you don't question it, only then can you be given that which cannot be questioned. Bhagwan Shree's words, sometimes, are to test you to see whether you will question. The outward manifestations of the initiation he gives are also to test you. His disciples are asked to wear ocher-colored robes continually and to wear around their necks a *mala*, a string of beads, to which a locket with his picture on it is attached. There are many esoteric reasons for this, which he explains in these discourses, but equally important, it seems, is that it is a gesture of surrender, a gesture of trust. Only if you trust can the master work with you.

In *I Am the Gate,* Bhagwan Shree explains how a twentieth-century enlightened master—a Buddha, a Christ, a Lao Tzu—works with his disciples, transforming them through methods that are as timeless as Bhagwan Shree's wisdom and as new as the poetry of his speech.

May his words make you dance, as they have made thousands of us dance. May they provoke you, prod you, confuse you, illuminate you, and haunt you. Then you can throw them. And only then, it seems, can the real work begin.

ma satya bharti

I Am the Gate

The Meaning of Initiation
and Discipleship

1

GOD IS WHAT IS HAPPENING

I apologize for asking personal questions. I ask not just for myself but for many. Who are you and why have you come into the world?

It makes no difference whether these questions are personal or not because to me the person does not exist. You cannot ask any personal questions because there is no one to be related to as a person. In fact, it is not presumptuous to ask personal questions, but to assume that a person *is* is certainly presumptuous. The person is nonexistent, a nonentity. In fact there is no person; or, there is only one person. Only God can be said to have a personality because only God can have a center.

We have no centers at all. The center in us is nonexistent, but we assume a center. This assumed center is the ego. The ego is hypothetical, illusory, but we feel that without a center life is not possible.

So you may think that these questions are personal, but insofar as the questions are directed toward me, they are directed toward a nonentity. As far as I am concerned, I do not feel that I am a person at all. The deeper one goes the less one is, and once someone reaches to the ultimate core of himself, there is no self at all.

Second, you ask who I am. I say, "I am not." I always tell seekers to ask, "Who am I?" not so that they will come to know who they are, but only in order that a moment will come when the question is asked so intensely that the questioner is not there, only the question remains. A moment is bound to come when the question is absolutely tense, as deep as it can go. Then the absurdity of it is revealed. You come to know that there is no one who can ask, "Who am I?" or who can be asked, "Who are you?" The question is asked not for an answer, but in order to transcend the question itself.

There is no one inside. In fact, there is no *inside* at all. And the moment the inside falls, there is also no outside; the moment you are inwardly *not,* there is no outwardness. Then the world becomes one whole, then existence is one whole—not divided into the dichotomy of "I" and "thou." So to me the question "Who are you?" makes no sense at all. Rather, "What is?" is the only relevant question. Not *who* but *what,* because the *what* can be the whole; it can be asked about the totality, about all that exists.

The question "What is?" is existential. There is no dichotomy in it; it does not divide. But the question "Who?" divides from the very start. It accepts the duality, the multiplicity of beings.

There is only being, not beings. When I say that there is only being, I mean that there is only beingness. The one cannot exist apart from the other. If there is no other, then to say that one exists is meaningless.

So there is not really being, only beingness. I always say that there is no God, there is only divineness, because the very word "God" carries a limitation around it, the very word "being" carries a finitude. It cannot be infinite. But beingness or divineness is infinite: it includes everything that is. It is all-inclusive; nothing is excluded.

So when you ask, "Who are you?" the question, to me, means, "What is?" But you have asked, through me, a very fundamental question.

"What is" is not "me," but being itself, existence itself. If one goes deeply into a single drop, one will find the ocean. Only on the surface is a drop just a drop. It is existence itself. So the ultimate nature of a single drop of water is that of the ocean. It is oceanic. Only in ignorance is one a drop of water. The moment one knows, one knows one is the ocean.

You have asked me a question about the drop, but to me it is a question about the ocean. So when I answer it, I am not answering about myself only but about you also. When I answer, I am not answering about me but about all that exists.

What exists? There are so many layers. If one is only aware of the surface, then matter exists: matter is the surface of existence. Earlier, science was only searching on the surface: only matter was thought to be real, nothing else. But now science has taken a step further. It says that matter is not, only energy is. Energy is the second layer. It is deeper than matter.

If one goes deep into matter then there is no matter, only energy. But that, too, is not enough because consciousness exists beyond energy. So when you ask, "Who are you?" I say, "I am consciousness," and this answer is all-inclusive. Everything is consciousness; I answer only as a representative of all.

You may not have heard that you are consciousness, you may not have known that you are consciousness, but I am answering even for you. Consciousness exists, and when I say something exists, it carries for me a particular meaning—that it will never be in nonexistence. If something can go into nonexistence it means that it never really existed. It was only phenomenal; it just *appeared* to exist.

All that changes is phenomenal; it is not really existential. Anything that changes is only on the surface. The innermost, the ultimate core, never changes. It is, and it is always in the present. You can never say it was, you can never say it will be. Whenever it is, it is. Only the present is applicable to it.

There is no past and no future, because the past and the future become relevant only when something changes. When something *is*, then there is no past and no future, but only the present. Of course, the meaning of "present" will be different, quite different.

For us, "present" means something that exists between the past and the future. But if there is no past and no future, then the present will be something quite different. It is not something between the past and the future. The present is just a moment, a moment between two nonexistentials: the past that has gone and is no more, and the future that has not yet come. Between these two nonexistentials, one present moment exists. But that is impossible. Between two nonexistentials there can be no existence. It only appears to be so.

When I say consciousness exists, I do not mean something concerned with the past and future, but something eternal. Not everlasting, because this word "everlasting" carries a sense of time. When I say that consciousness always exists in the present, I mean it is nontemporal. It is beyond time and, simultaneously, beyond space, because all that is in space will become nonexistential and, similarly, all that is in time will become nonexistential. Time and space are not two things; that is why I relate them. They are one. Time is only a dimension of space. The "movement in space" is time and "nonmoving time" is space. Existence is nontemporal, nonspatial.

I think you will be able to understand me now when I say that I am someone who is nontemporal and nonspatial. But my "I" is all-inclusive. You are included, the questioner is included. Nothing is excluded in my "I." Now it will be easier to answer your inquiry.

Everything that changes is purposive. There is something to be done—it exists for a purpose—and the moment the purpose is fulfilled, it goes into nonexistence. But all that is really existential is nonpurposive. There is no purpose to life that can be fulfilled. And if there is any purpose and it is fulfilled, then existence will become meaningless.

So only temporal things have purposes. They are meant for something. You can say it in this way: they are means to some end. That is what is meant by purposive—they exist for something to be fulfilled. The moment it is fulfilled they cease to exist. But "I" will be needed always—and when I say "I," it is all-inclusive.

There is no purpose to life; existence is nonpurposive. That is why it is called a *leela*, a play. Existence itself has no purpose to fulfill. It is not going anywhere—there is no end that it is moving toward—but still it is moving, still much is happening. That is why it must be only a *leela*, a play of outflowing energy.

Once you know that you are part of cosmic consciousness, you realize that there is no purpose. Your existence is a play. Of course, the play becomes cosmic, multidimensional—you do much—but, still, there is no doer and there is no purpose. These two things are not there. It is just a play.

This must be noted: a doer cannot exist without a purpose and a purpose cannot exist without a doer. They are two polarities of one ego. The ego feels very uncomfortable if there is no purpose; it is fulfilled through purposes. Something is to be done; one can succeed in doing it. One is to reach somewhere, one is to do something—one has to make a name for oneself—so the ego is purposive.

Existence, on the other hand, is not purposive. And unless you know what is beyond the ego, beyond purpose, you have not known anything at all.

To me, everything is just a play. Neither "I am" nor is there any purpose. Yet things are happening. You may ask why they are happening. They are happening because there is no purpose in stopping them and there is no one to stop them. Do you understand me? There is no one to stop them and there is no purpose in stopping them. It is in the nature of things for them to happen.

If you can just allow what is happening to happen, you become a passage. If you are active you cannot be a passage, you cannot be a medium. Only passivity makes you a medium. Passivity means that you are not; it is not just a verbal passivity. The ego is always active, so the moment you are passive, the ego is not. Passivity means egolessness.

I am totally passive. Whatsoever happens, happens. I never question why, because there is no one to be asked. Even if you find God somewhere, He will just laugh at the question. Even He cannot answer it. He cannot answer it because existence has no causality.

"Why?" is meaningful only in division. If there is a beginning and an end then causality becomes meaningful, but if you understand the whole flux as endless, beginningless, then everything dissolves into something else and everything comes from something else, just like waves in the ocean. Every wave has another wave behind it and another wave in front of it. The ocean is wave after wave; the waves are eternal.

Only human beings ask, "Why?" so only human beings are in anxiety. When the human mind becomes anxious, it creates questions and then supplies the answers. Because the questions are meaningless, the answers are even more so. But we cannot be at ease unless we find the answers to our fabricated questions, so we go on finding answers and creating new questions.

If you can see the whole nonsense of asking questions and then answering them, you will see that you are just carrying on a monologue with yourself. Even if you are asking and I am answering, it is the human mind asking and the human mind answering. It is just a hide-and-seek game of the same mind. It makes no difference who is asking and who is answering. The human mind questions and the human mind answers.

We have created a confusion of questions and answers, but not a single question has been answered. The questions remain where they always were. If you can see this whole profusion of questions and answers, this meaningless, fruitless effort leading nowhere—if, like a flash of lightning, you become aware of this whole nonsense—then you can laugh at the absurdity of the human mind. And the moment there is laughter, you transcend the human mind completely. Then there is no question and there is no answer. Then you simply live: there is no purpose and there is no cause. Then living itself is enough.

You ask me and I answer you, but I myself cannot ask any questions. As far as I am concerned there is no answer and there is no question. I go on living just like the waves in the ocean, or the leaves of a tree, or the clouds in the sky—without any question and without any answer. The moment I became aware of this whole absurdity of questions, something fell down completely, totally. It was a resurrection. I was reborn, reborn in a cosmic dimension, not as an "I," but as cosmic consciousness itself.

In this cosmic dimension, everything is a play. Once you realize that everything is just a play, you are completely at ease, absolutely at ease. Then there is no tension, you are relaxed.

Then there is no ego. The ego cannot relax; it lives on tensions, it feeds on tensions. When there is no ego, there is no tension. Then you are all-inclusive: there is no past and there is no future. You are eternity. Then anything that happens is a happening. It is not that you are doing it; it is not that something is to be fulfilled through you. These are all illusory notions.

Even a religious person may think in terms of doing something. Then the ego has become settled, pious—and more dangerous. If the ego is there, both the doer and the doing are there. Only the object has changed; the process is the same.

To me—and when I refer to "me," there is no one who is being referred to. It is only a linguistic device in order for you to understand what I am saying. In fact, there is no one who can be referred to as "me" or "you," but then language will be impossible. That is why truth cannot be expressed in language. Truth cannot take on any linguistic form because language is created by the ego. It comes out of the ego, so it can never transcend ego. Even if you know that there is no one who can be referred to as "me," you have to use it when you speak. But remember, when I say "me" there is no one who is being referred to.

As far as I am concerned, as far as this "me" is concerned, nothing is to be done. Things happen by themselves. We ourselves happen; we *are* happenings. The whole existence is a happening, not a doing. It would be better if I say that the old concept of God as the creator is not meaningful to me. I will not say, "God the creator," because the expression simply reflects our egoistic conception of creation, of doing. Just as we do something, we conceive of a God who has made the world. We project ourselves onto the cosmic plane so we think in terms of a creator and the creation. We create a dichotomy.

To me, "God" is what happens, not the creator. "God" means

that which goes on happening eternally, so anything that happens is God. You and everyone are happenings, and this eternal happening is God. There is no creator and no creation. The very dichotomy is egoistic; it is our projecting of ourselves onto the cosmic plane. Once you know that there is no dichotomy within yourself between the doer and the doing, you know that within existence itself there is no doer and no doing, only happenings. Once you have this revelation of eternal happenings, there is no burden, there is no tension. Your birth is a happening and your death will be a happening. Your being here is a happening; your not being here will be a happening.

From where does this ego come which thinks, "I am. I am doing"? It comes through memory. Your memory goes on recording happenings: you are born, you are a child; then youth comes, then you are old. Things happen: love happens, hatred happens, and the memory goes on recording it. When you look at the past, the whole accumulated memory becomes your "I."

I loved someone. It would be better, and more exact, to say that somewhere love happened. "I" was not the doer. Love has happened just as birth happens, just as death happens. If a person can remember this for only twenty-four hours—that things are happening and there is no doer—he will not be the same again.

But it is very arduous to remember, even for a single moment. It is very difficult to remember that events are happening and you are not the doer. For example, I am speaking. If I say that I am speaking and I mean that "I" am speaking, then I have misinterpreted the phenomenon. I am speaking, speaking is happening through me, but I do not know what the next sentence will be. When it comes you will know it and I will also know it. It is a happening, something comes through me. I am not at all a doer; something happens in me.

This is what is meant when we say that the Vedas are impersonal, that they were not created by persons. We mean by this that those who compiled the Vedas knew this fact: the fact that something was happening through them, they were not the doers. Something was coming to them. They were only the passage, the medium, the vehicle. And even this "being a vehicle" was a happening. It was not their doing that they became vehicles— otherwise the same fallacy would be there on another level.

Go deep into any of your acts and you will find a happening there. There will be no act because there is no actor. Then you cannot ask, "Why?" because who will ask and who can answer? No one can answer because no one is there to answer. The house is vacant, the owner is not there. Let things go on happening. The house itself, without the owner, is capable of allowing the happenings.

Try to understand it more clearly. Buddha said so many times, "When we walk, there is no walker—only the walk." How can this be understood? If I am not, how can I walk? Walk and try to find out where you are. You will find only the walk.

You cannot understand how someone can say that there is speaking and no speaker. But if you go deeply into the act of speaking, you will find that no speaker is there, just the speaking. In fact, there have been no poets—poetry has happened. There have been no painters—it's only that painting has been happening. But because of the ego, the vehicle becomes the owner.

Memory creates the fallacy. But the fallacy does not exist for me. Memory cannot trap me, it has lost its grip on me. So everything happens, but there is no doer. All that will happen, will happen. I will not be the cause of it, I will not be the master.

Once you know that you are not, you become a master in a very different sense. If you are not, then you cannot be made a slave. Now your freedom is total; no one can make you a slave. Now there can be neither slavery nor any possibility of it. It is paradoxical but it is a fact that one who tries to be a master is always in danger of becoming a slave, and one who loses himself—his mastery, his efforts, his doing—is beyond slavery. He is free, as free as the sky. He is freedom itself.

So if you like, I can say that I am freedom. There is no reason for this freedom because if there was any reason then I would not be free. I would be bound to the reason, tethered to the reason.

If there was anything that had to be done in order to be free then I would be tethered to it, I would not be free. I am absolute freedom in the sense that nothing is to be done. I am an awaiting. Things will happen and I will accept them. And if they do not happen, then I will accept the nonhappening and I will go on waiting.

This waiting makes one a medium of the divine forces of existence. Much is done through you when the doer is not, and nothing is done through you when the doer is there. When the doer is there, you are—you are doing something. But it is impossible to do something: doing is not possible, a doer is not possible. You are engaged in an absurd effort and only frustration will be the result.

When you are not, you always succeed. There can be no failure because you have never thought of being anything. If failure happens, it is a happening; if success happens, it is a happening. When you know that either success or failure is a happening, not a doing, you become indifferent. Whichever one happens makes no difference; either one will do.

When I say, "I," everyone is included in that "I." I am consciousness and I am freedom. I use two words—consciousness and freedom—only to make the mystery more understandable for you. Both have the same meaning. Consciousness is freedom and freedom is consciousness. The more material, the less free. If I say this table is material, I mean to say that it is not free to move. If I say you are a conscious being, I mean that you are free to some extent. But if you become consciousness itself, if you go deep, to the very source of existence, you are totally free.

I know that you are consciousness itself, not just conscious beings. Consciousness is not a quality attached to you. You *are* consciousness, you are totally free. So you can proceed from anywhere. Either be more free or be more conscious, and the other will result automatically.

Be more free and you will be more conscious. Be more conscious and you will be more free. You cannot be otherwise because consciousness creates freedom. When you are absolutely conscious you are absolutely free. Then there is no cause and no purpose for you to exist. Then everything is a happening. And a happening is a *leela*.

Bhagwan, are you self-realized? What is your relationship to the whole and what is your relationship to people?

The word "self-realized" is not right, because realization always means a transcendence of the self. The word "self-realization" is therefore contradictory. If you realize, you know that there is no self. If you do not realize, then there is a self. Selfhood is nonrealization and realization is nonselfhood. So I cannot say that I am self-realized. I can only say that now there is no self.

There was a self, but it was there only as far as the door. The moment you enter the temple of realization, the self is no longer there. It is a shadow that follows you to the door. And it not only follows you, but clings to you.

But only up to the door. It cannot enter the temple. If you want to save it, you will have to remain outside. The self is the last thing one has to throw. One can throw everything, but to throw the self is almost impossible because the effort toward self-realization is an effort of the self *for* the self. But the moment you realize, *you* will not be.

Because you do not want to lose the self, all the great teachers have used words that are false. "Self-realization" is a false word, but you will not understand if they say "no-self realization." It will become absurd. But that is the real thing: no-self realization. Buddha used the word *anatta*, no-self.

Anatta. Only Buddha used this word. That is why Buddhism was uprooted from India. Buddhism could not establish roots until it began to use the word "self-realization." The word came to be used by Buddhists in China and Japan, but Buddha himself used "no-self realization."

I am also using "no-self realization." That is the only realization. The moment there is no self, you have become cosmic.

It is not that there is something to be realized. To know the self is the only—no doubt the greatest, the ultimate—game. The self is not something to be protected; it is something to be destroyed. It is something that is the barrier toward your ultimate potentiality, toward your ultimate realization.

So I cannot say that I am self-realized. I can only say that I am no-self realized. That is the only realization that is possible, no other realization exists. The emphasis of all who claim self-realization is on the self and not on realization. My emphasis is on realization. That is why I emphatically deny the self.

How am I related to the totality and to other people?

Relationship exists between two selves, so for me there can be no relationship. Relationship always exists between two. In every relationship you remain ultimately unrelated because duality remains. Relationship is only a façade to hide the duality. For a moment you delude yourself into thinking that you are related, but then suddenly *you* are there again. The duality is revealed and there is no relationship.

When we are in love we appear to be related. We create the fallacy of relationship, but, in fact, we are just deceiving ourselves. The two will remain two. However close, the two will always remain two. Even in sexual communion there will be two. The twoness only creates a fallacy of oneness. Oneness can never exist between two selves; oneness can exist only between two non-selves.

So as far as I am concerned, I am not related to the cosmic reality, not related at all. By that I do not mean that I am isolated. I mean that there is no one to be related to the whole. I am one with the whole and the whole is one with me. Nothing exists outside of me; there is no duality.

There is nothing that is "other" to me, so from my side, relationship is not possible. But as far as other people are concerned, relationship is possible. Someone is related to me as a friend, someone else is related as an enemy, someone else as a brother, someone else as a disciple. They may be related to me, but I am not related to them.

The whole thing that is happening through me is to make them also unrelated. But this cannot be done through any effort on their part; it can come about only through no-self realization. If one knows that there is no one who can be a disciple and no one who can be a guru, if one knows that there is no one who can be related to anyone—only then does the self fall and one's emptiness is revealed. Then you are naked; there are no clothes to give you a boundary, a self.

In your total nakedness—when you know that there is no self —you know that you are nothing but emptiness, an inner sky. Then you become one with the whole. Then you are really related, but then there is no relationship. When there is no self to exist in relationship, oneness happens.

You have asked me how I am related to the whole and how I am related to other people. To me these are not two things. The cosmic happens in many ways: the sun, the stars, the earth; trees, animals, people. Only frequencies differ, the divinity is the same. So to me the cosmic is not something separate from human beings.

You are related to me because you *are*. Until you are *not*, you will be related. This creates a very difficult situation.

You feel yourself to be related to me; you feel that you belong to me. Then you begin to expect that I should belong to you. Because you feel that you are related to me, you begin to expect that I should feel related to you. Because of that expectation I know you are bound to be frustrated. Even if you feel related to a person who is a self, it is bound to be frustrating, but there may be a time-gap before the frustration sets in. With a person who is a no-self, there will not even be a time-gap. Every moment will be frustrating because there will be no fulfillment of your expectations. There is no one to fulfill them.

So I am very irresponsible because there is no one who can be responsible. There are responses, but there is no one who is responsible. Each response, therefore, is atomic; it cannot be sequential. With me, you cannot expect anything to be continuous from one moment to the next. Even I do not know what will happen next. My response is going to be complete in itself—not in any way related to the past or to the future.

The ego consists of a series of events, happenings, and memories, one thing following from the next in sequence. But if you expect me to act sequentially, it will be difficult for you. That is why everyone will feel angry with me at some time or other. My response is always from the moment, not from the past.

A response that is continuous with the past becomes a responsibility. Then you can rely upon the other. I am very unreliable, you can never rely on me. I myself cannot rely on me! I do not know what is going to happen; I am completely open and accepting of anything that happens. And I never think in terms of relationship; I cannot. I live in oneness with everything that is.

Whenever you are near me, it does not mean that I am related to you. Rather, I become one with you. This oneness you interpret as love, but it is neither love nor hate. All that is known as love can change into hatred at any moment, but this oneness can never change into hate. You may be near, you may be far; you may be a friend, you may be an enemy—it makes no difference. As far as I am concerned, you can come to me or you can go from me. It makes no difference!

Relationship is conditional; oneness is nonconditional. Relationship always exists with conditions. If the conditions change, the relationship will change. Every relationship is always in a wavering state—always dying, always changing. Every relationship creates fear because there is always the danger of the relationship being broken. The more fear there is, the more you cling; and the more you cling, the more fear you create.

Oneness is diametrically opposite to this. It is unconditional. It does not exist because of any condition, any expectation, any fulfillment, or any future result that is hoped for. It is neither conditioned by the past nor oriented to the future. It is momentary, atomic—unrelated to the past, unrelated to the future.

I feel a oneness with people and a oneness with the whole cosmos. The cosmos feels the same oneness toward me as I feel toward it. I did not always feel this oneness, but now I know that the cosmos has always been feeling this oneness toward me. Oneness is always flowing; it has always been flowing. Now I feel a oneness toward the cosmic and I also feel it toward people.

The moment someone feels this oneness toward me, he becomes part of the cosmic. Then he is not a person, he becomes cosmic. Once you feel oneness with even one person you have known the taste of ecstasy. Then you can jump into the all. This is what is happening around me. I am not doing it; it is happening around me.

I call you near to me just to give you a taste of oneness. If you can realize this oneness even for a single moment, then you will never be the same again. But you must wait for the happening very patiently. It is unknown, unpredictable. No one can say when the moment of happening is near.

Sometimes your mind is so tuned that you can feel the oneness. That is why I insist on meditation. It is nothing but a tuning of the mind to such a peak that you can jump into oneness. Meditation, to me, means tuning the mind toward oneness, opening the mind toward oneness.

This can only happen when your meditation has gone beyond you; otherwise it can never happen. If it is less than you, if you are doing it, you are the controller. Then it cannot happen—because you are the barrier.

I persuade you to move into meditation because, beyond certain limits, you will not be. Meditation will take you over; by and by you will be pushed. Of course you will have to begin the meditation—there is no other way—but you will not end the meditation. You will begin it, but you will not end it. Somewhere in between, the happening will happen. You will be thrown, and the meditation will be there. Then you will be tuned to the infinite, then you will be tuned to the cosmic—then you will be one with the whole.

Oneness is important, not relationship. Relationship is *sansar*, relationship is the world. Because of relationship you have to be born again and again. Once you have known oneness, there is no birth and there is no death. Then there is no one except you—

everything is included in you; you have become the cosmic. The individual must go before there is oneness. Before the divine comes, the ego must go.

The ego is the source of all relationship. The world is relationship; God is not a relationship, the divine is not a relationship. The divine has no self so you cannot be related to it. A *bhakta*, a devotee, can never reach the divine because he thinks in terms of relationship: God the father, God the lover, God the beloved. He thinks in terms of relationship; he goes on thinking of God as the other. Then he is something separate from God. The self is there; the ego is there. He can never transcend ego.

This is very subtle. The devotee is always struggling to surrender. Devotion, the path of devotion, is the path of surrender. The devotee is trying to surrender, but if you try to surrender to someone, the other is there. The other cannot exist if you are not, so if the other is there, *you* are there. You go on existing. You exist in the shadows, you forget yourself, but forgetting yourself is not surrender. You remember the divine so much that you cannot remember yourself, but you are still there in the background. As long as God is the other, as long as God is something separate from you, you are still there. So the path of devotion, as it exists, cannot lead you to the transcendental, to the cosmic, to oneness.

To me it is not a question of surrendering to someone. It is just a question of surrendering the self. Not surrendering at someone's feet, just surrendering yourself. If there is no self, then you have become one with the whole.

The self can go on creating deceptions. The greatest deception is the deception of devotion to God. Any deception that is religious can be dangerous because then to deny it will create guilt. You will feel guilty if you deny selfhood to the divine, but the selfhood of the divine is just a projection of your own selfhood. The moment you are no-self, God is selfless, the whole existence has become selfless. And when the whole existence has become selfless, you are one with it.

Selflessness is the path. Selflessness is the real devotion; selflessness is the authentic surrender. The problem is always of the self.

Even if you think of liberation, *moksha*, you think of freedom of the self, not freedom from the self. You think that you will be free. You cannot be free; *moksha* is not freedom of the self, but freedom from the self. *Moksha* is selflessness. I am not a self, nor is anyone else a self.

But we deceive ourselves. It is as if each wave in the ocean conceives itself as something separate from the ocean. It appears to be separate; it can deceive itself that it is separate. There are so many waves around and each wave appears different. My wave is higher than yours or lower than yours—how can they be the same? Waves cannot look deep down in the ocean; only the surface is known. Your wave is dying and my wave is young and rising; your wave has reached the shore and I am far away. So how can I think that we are both the same? But whether we think so or not, we are the same.

The wave that you are addressing, the wave that is known as "me," is not an ego, it is not a self. It has known the ocean. The wave is just a surface phenomenon—an appearance, a movement. This wave that I call "I" knows that it is the ocean, that the ocean is the real. Your wave is not separate from it.

I have known that which joins all. You may call it self-realization; I will not. I will call it no-self realization because no-selfness is the essence of all realization. But I think you understand what I mean.

What I have said may not be what I mean, and what I mean may not be what I have said. Do not confuse my sayings with my meanings; always look deeply into what I have said. Always listen to that which has not been said but indicated. There are things that cannot be said. They must be shown, indicated. All that is deep and all that is ultimate can only be shown, never said. So do not think about my words. Always throw the words; they are meaningless. Then go deep down to the wordless meaning, to the silent meaning. It is always there behind the words.

Words are always dead; the meaning is always alive. Through words you can become open to the wordless, but you can never become open through intellectual understanding. You can only be open with your total being, not with your intellect alone. It is not that the intellect sometimes misunderstands. Rather, the intellect always misunderstands. It is not that the intellect sometimes errs; it is that intellect is the error. It always errs.

Whatsoever is being said, be sympathetic to it, do not try to understand it. Let it go deep inside you. Be vulnerable to it, open to it. Let it go deep into the heart; do not create intellectual barriers to it. Then when your full being is participating, you will know. You may not understand, but you will know.

Understanding is not enough; knowing is needed. Sometimes you understand, or think that you have understood. Then a barrier to knowing is created. The intellect understands; the being knows. The intellect is just a part. It is your being that is real.

When you know, you know with your blood, you know with your bones, you know with your heart. If you understand, you understand only with the mechanism of the mind, which is not so deep. Mind is only a device, a utilitarian device that is needed to survive. It is needed if you are to relate to others, but it becomes a barrier toward oneness—toward spiritual death and resurrection. It is only a device to survive; it is not meant to reveal the ultimate truth, it is not a means to know the hidden mysteries.

So do not think about what I am saying. Go home and sleep on it. Just let it move inside. Let it penetrate you. Do not guard yourself; be open. Only when what I am saying has reached your innermost being will it be known and understood.

That is what is meant by *shraddha,* faith. Faith does not mean belief. Belief is intellectual: one can believe intellectually; one can disbelieve intellectually. Both are intellectual. Faith is not belief; faith is not intellectual at all. It is a total participation; it is being one with the hidden mysteries. It is a jump.

I am not interested in theories at all; I am not interested in philosophies at all. I am interested in the existential jump. When I say something, it is only to lead you to what cannot be said. When I use words, I use them only to lead you toward silence; when I assert something, it is only to indicate the unassertable.

My words are not really to express something, but to indicate the inexpressible.

Listen sympathetically, because only sympathy can be the opening. Let whatever I have said drop into you so it can flower. If the seed goes into the depths, there will be a flowering, and when the flower comes, you will know what has been said without being said. You will know what has been said, but yet remains unsaid.

2
Sannyas: Renunciation through Positive Growth

Bhagwan, why do you give sannyas *to almost everybody who comes to you? What is your concept of* sannyas *and what obligations does it involve? Lastly, how will your* sannyas, *and your* sannyasins, *affect the world?*

To me, *sannyas* is not something very serious. Life itself is not very serious, and one who is serious is always dead. Life is just an overflowing energy without any purpose, and to me *sannyas* is to live life purposelessly, to live life as a play and not as a work.

The serious mind—the so-called serious mind, which is diseased—converts play into work. *Sannyasins* are to do the very opposite: to convert work into play. If you can take this whole life as just a dream, a dream act, then you are a *sannyasin.*

One who considers life to be a dream, a dream-drama, has renounced. Renunciation is not leaving the world, but changing your attitude toward the world. That is why I can initiate anyone into *sannyas.* To me, initiation itself is play. I do not ask for any qualifications—whether you are qualified or not—because qualifications are asked when something serious is to be done. Just by being part of the existence, everyone is qualified enough to play. He can play, and even if he is unqualified it makes no difference because the whole thing is just a play.

And that is why I do not ask for any qualifications. Nor does my *sannyas* involve any obligation. The moment you are a *sannyasin* you are totally free.

Sannyas means that now you have made a decision—and this is the last decision. Now you do not have to make any more decisions. You have made your last decision: to live in indecision, to live in freedom.

One who lives through decision, through choice, can never be free. He is always bound by the past, bound by decisions he has made in the past. The moment you are initiated into *sannyas*, you are initiated into an uncharted future—unplanned. Now you are not tethered to the past; you are free to live moment to moment. Now you can act, you can play, you can allow whatever is happening to you to happen. Now you live in insecurity.

To renounce your name, to renounce your property, is not really to move into insecurity. It is a very superficial insecurity. The mind that was thinking of the property as security remains the same. Property is no security at all; you will die even with all your property. A home is no security at all; you can die in it. The false notion that property, home, friends, and family are security still prevails in the mind that thinks, "I have renounced. Now I am living in insecurity." Only a person who lives untethered to the past lives in insecurity.

Insecurity means to be untethered to the past. This has so many meanings, because all you know comes from the past. Even your mind is part of the past, so one who renounces knowledge is really renouncing something.

You yourself come from the past. You are nothing but the accumulation of your experiences. So one who renounces *himself* is renouncing something. All your desires, all your hopes, all your expectations confirm the past. One who renounces his past renounces his desires, his hopes, his expectations.

Now you will be just like an emptiness, a nothingness, a nobody. *Sannyas* means throwing all claims of being somebody. Now you are moving into nonidentity, into nobodiness. *Sannyas* is the last decision of your mind. Now the past is closed; the identification with the past is broken. The continuity is not there: you are new; you are reborn.

And everyone who is alive is qualified. Everyone who is alive is qualified to live in insecurity. If one is really to live, one has to live in insecurity. Every effort to be secure is a renunciation of life. The more secure you are, the less alive. The more secure, the more dead and vice versa. For example, a dead man cannot die, so he is death-proof; a dead man cannot be ill, so he is disease-proof. A dead man is so secure that those who go on living may seem foolish to him! They live in insecurity. If you are alive at all, you are insecure. The more insecure, the more alive. So a *sannyasin*, to me, is a person who decides to live to the utmost, to the optimum, to the maximum. He is like a flame burning from both ends.

There is no obligation to my *sannyas,* and there is no commitment. You are not bound to any discipline. If you want to call insecurity a discipline, that is another matter. But of course, it is an inner discipline.

This does not mean that you are going to be anarchic, no. Anarchy is always bound up with the order, with the system. If you renounce order, you can never be disorderly. It is not denying order; it is just renouncing. If you renounce order, renounce rules, then to be orderly is just an act, a game that you play for the sake of others. You will not be serious about it; it is just a rule of the game. You walk to the left or you walk to the right for others' sake, for the sake of traffic, not that there is anything serious about it. Nothing is serious in it; it is just play.

So a *sannyasin* is not going to be disorderly. But as far as he himself is concerned, as far as his inner consciousness is concerned, now there will be no order. This does not mean there will be disorder. Disorder is always a part of order; when there is order, there is always the possibility of disorder. When there is no order, then there is no disorder; there is just spontaneity. Moment to moment you live, moment to moment you act. Each moment is complete in itself. You do not decide for it; you do not make a decision how to act. The moment comes to you, and you act. There is no predetermination; there is no preplan.

The moment comes to you. Whatever happens, you allow. And the more spontaneous you are, the more you shall feel a new discipline arising in you, a moment-to-moment discipline.

This is very different from what we normally mean by discipline, so it will be better to understand it clearly. When you decide what to do beforehand, it is because you do not think you are conscious enough to act in the moment, spontaneously. You are not self-confident; that is why you decide beforehand. But still you are deciding. If you cannot act in the moment, how can you decide beforehand? In fact, when the moment comes you will be more experienced; now you are less experienced. Tomorrow you will be richer, so why decide today for tomorrow?

When you decide something beforehand, it carries no meaning. It will only be destructive. You decide today and act tomorrow. Now everything has changed: everything is new and the decision is old. You are new—the moment is new—and the decision is old.

And if you do not act according to the decision you made beforehand, you feel guilty. All those who teach you to decide beforehand create guilt. If you do not act according to yesterday's decision you feel guilty, and if you do, you will not be able to act adequately and frustration will follow.

So when I tell you not to commit yourself to any decision, it is so that you will be free. Each moment, let each act come to you and let your total being decide. Let the decision come as the act happens—in the moment. Never let your decision precede the act or the act can never be total.

When you decide beforehand, you decide intellectually. Your total being can never be in it because the moment itself has not come. If I love someone and I decide that when I meet him or her I will act this way—I will say this; I will do this and will not do that—this can only be intellectual, mental. This can never be total because the moment has not arrived. The total being has not been challanged, so how can the total being act?

If I have decided how to act, when the moment comes my total being will not be able to act because the decision will be there. I will only imitate, follow, copy, the decision I had made before. I will be false. I will not be real because I will not be total. I will have a blueprint of how to act and I will act according to it. This will be a mental act, not an act of the total being. Whether I succeed or I fail—in either case I will have failed because my total being was not in it. I will not feel the love I had anticipated feeling.

Let the moment come to you fresh; don't decide beforehand. Let the moment challenge you; let your total being act. Then the act is total; then you are totally in it. The best that is possible will happen out of this totality, never out of decisions made beforehand.

So *sannyas* means living moment to moment, with no commitments from the past. If I give you a *mala* to wear and I give you new clothes, this is only for your remembrance: to remind you that now you do not have to make any more decisions. It is to make you remember that now you are not the old.

When this awareness becomes so deep that you do not need to remember it, then throw the robe, throw the *mala*. If it comes to you to drop them, then drop them. Do not make a decision to drop them; just drop them.

Do not make the wearing of the *mala* or the wearing of ocher robes a commitment to me. If it comes to you to throw them, then throw them. But not until your awareness of yourself as a *sannyasin* has become so deep that now, even in sleep, you know that you are a *sannyasin*.

When your ocher robe is there even in your dreams, then throw it; then it is meaningless. If even the unconscious remembers it, if you cannot forget it in any situation, then there is no need to wear it. The wearing of an ocher robe is just a device to help you: to help you toward freedom, to help you toward total being, to help you toward total action.

I go on giving *sannyas* to each and everybody who happens to be with me even for a single moment. I do not know about tomorrow at all, so I cannot wait. If you come to me this moment, then whatever is to be done is to be done this moment. I cannot wait because I do not know about tomorrow, about what is going to happen. I cannot plan. So the moment you are with me, whatever is to be done must be done. It cannot be postponed because, for me, there is no future. Only this moment exists.

My *sannyas* is not the traditional *sannyas*. It is a totally new concept—or a totally ancient one that has been forgotten completely. You can call it either: it is the newest and the oldest simultaneously. Whenever there has been a real *sannyas* it has been like this, but there have always been imitations and imitators. You cannot prevent it; there will always be imitators. They make everything into a discipline because only a discipline can be imitated.

Sannyas is something that cannot be imitated; freedom cannot be imitated. *Sannyas* can never be imitated, but what can those who are imitators do but try to imitate it? They will try to make a system out of it—imitators always create systems—because only a system can be imitated; freedom cannot be imitated.

Life, as it is normally lived, is nothing but imitation. Imitation goes on and on; the whole world is imitating. Your whole upbringing is through imitation. It may be language, it may be morality, it may be society, it may be culture—everything is learned through imitation; everything is imbibed through imitation.

Imitation is successful everywhere except in *sannyas*. There, imitation destroys much. It is not as destructive anywhere else because everywhere else imitation is the rule. You cannot be free with language, you must imitate it; you cannot be free with the social structure, you must imitate it; imitation succeeds everywhere. Only in *sannyas*—the dimension of total freedom—is imitation destructive, because the very dimension of *sannyas* is diametrically opposite to imitation.

Imitation will destroy the authentic *sannyas*. Jesus is imitated;

there is even a book called *Imitation of Christ.* Whenever *sannyas* is imitated, nothing of the real *sannyas* is left.

So when I say that there is no commitment to my *sannyas,* I mean that there is nothing to be done, nothing to be imitated. There are no rules to follow. You are totally free. I throw you into an openness.

That is what is meant by initiation. It is not narrowing you down; it is giving you an open sky. It is pushing you so that you can fly in an open sky. Of course, there are no routes and no road maps; there cannot be. There cannot be any path through the sky; you have to fly alone, you have to depend on yourself alone. Your own existence will be your sole company, the only company.

Life is just like the open sky. It is not like a path on the earth; you cannot follow it. Following is impossible; you have to go alone. Initiation means that now I push you into the aloneness. Now you are totally alone, not depending on anyone, not even me.

It requires courage. To imitate is easy; to follow is easy; to depend on someone is easy. But to be totally alone—with no map, no discipline, no system—requires the greatest courage. A *sannyasin* means one who is courageous. This courage is not something that can be imitated; it has to be developed through living. You will err, you will go astray—that is implied in it. But by erring you will learn, and by going astray you will come to what is right. There is no other way. You have to pass through many difficulties. This walking alone, this flying alone—one has to pass through this austerity.

My *sannyas* is different in another sense also. The old *sannyas* —the so-called *sannyas* that is prevalent today—is less a spiritual renunciation and more a social renunciation. The whole emphasis of it is more physiological than spiritual.

My *sannyas,* on the other hand, is basically spiritual, so you can be a *sannyasin* anywhere, wherever you are. It demands no superficial changes; it demands only a transformed mind. It demands involvement: deep, inner, spiritual involvement.

As I see it, the more you are involved physiologically, the less possibility there is to go deeply within. Once involved with the physiological you will never be out of it because of certain intrinsic impossibilities. For example, if someone is trying to be above desires, he is struggling for something that is impossible. Desires are natural, your body cannot exist without them. You can go on working with the body, but desires will still be there. They will be less, of course, but they will be there. The weaker the body, the less desires will be strongly felt, so you can go on weakening the body, but unless you die, the body will continue to have desires.

The body not only has desires; it has needs. These needs have to be fulfilled, and the better fulfilled, the less they trouble you; the less they demand, the less time is needed for them. So if you are struggling with your physiological needs, you will waste your whole life.

This whole process of struggle of the old *sannyas* is negative. It is fighting against something. Of course, it is ego-strengthening; whenever you fight, the ego is strengthened. If you can kill a desire, you become more egoistic; if you can deny your body a particular need, you become more egoistic. Fight is always ego-satisfying, ego-fulfilling.

My *sannyas* is something positive, not something negative. It is not to deny your bodily needs; it is not to deny your superficial needs. It is to develop, to grow in your inwardness. It is not fighting against something; it is helping all your energies to grow toward something. Your being must grow and become mature. And the more your being grows, the less you will be an ego.

Once your being has grown, you know what is a need and what is a desire. Otherwise you can never make a distinction between needs and desires. A desire is always mad; a need is always sensible. If you deny your needs you are suicidal, and if you go on increasing your desires, then you are again being suicidal. Both are suicidal. If you go on denying your needs, you are committing suicide, and if you go on increasing your desires, you are committing suicide in a different way.

If your desires become too strong, if they become overwhelming, you will become mad. The tension will be unbearable. If you deny your needs, you again create an unbearable tension. So there are two types of suicidal minds: one that goes on denying its needs and one that goes on transforming its simple needs into complex desires.

The distinction between desires and needs can never be made outwardly. No one else can decide for you what is a desire and what is a need. Only your own awareness can be the measure. Something may be a need to someone, and to another it may be a desire, so no ready-made answer can be given.

Only this much can be said: the minimum definition of a need is that without which you cannot exist. But one's own awareness will ultimately decide—and that, too, cannot be decided forever, because something may be a need today and a desire tomorrow. This moment it is a need and the next moment it may be a desire. But once there is a positive awareness in you—once you are aware of your mind and its cunning ways; once you are aware of your ego and its methods of strengthening itself, its methods of feeding itself—you will know the distinction.

So I am not negative. *Sannyas*—my neo-*sannyas*—is absolutely positive. It is to enable something to grow within you. I am trying to give you a positive attitude toward your being, not a negative attitude. You are not to deny anything. But, of course, many things may be denied—not by you, but automatically—because as you go more inward, you will shrink outwardly. It is bound to happen.

The less one is inwardly a being, the more he has to substitute for this outwardly. He will go on spreading out. But do not struggle with your spreading, outward self. Work with the inner seed that is you, so it can grow to such heights that this outward nonsense will automatically fall down. Once you know the inner riches, there is nothing that is comparable to it in the outside world. Once you know the inner bliss, then enjoyment is foolish; then all that goes by the name of entertainment is foolish, stupid. It just falls down. Once you know the inner ecstasy, you know that all that is known as happiness, joy, is nothing but deception. But you cannot know it beforehand. Unless you have known the inner happiness, you cannot say this. And if you say it, you are just deceiving yourself.

Sannyas, as a positive attitude, is something altogether different from the traditional *sannyas.* You can remain where you are, you can go on doing whatever you are doing. No outward change is asked for. Of course, there will be changes, but they will come by themselves. Let them come when they come, but do not try to make them come. Do not make any effort, do not force them to come.

And I see more possibility in the world that is coming for a positive *sannyas,* for positive renunciation. The negative concept of *sannyas,* of denying oneself, was previously possible for so many reasons. One was the way in which society was structured. Agricultural societies could allow persons, some persons, to be completely without work. But the more a society is industrialized, the less possibility there is of joint families. A loose economic structure could allow for joint families, but with a more planned economy, there is less possibility of joint families. Now *sadhus* and monks seem to be exploiters. They cannot be respected; they cannot be allowed to exist.

As I see it, everyone must do whatever he can do. One must contribute to the society in which one lives; one should not remain an exploiter. A religious person cannot be an exploiter. If even a religious person exploits, then we cannot expect others not to exploit.

To me, a *sannyasin* will not be an exploiter. He will earn a living; he will be a producer, not only a consumer. A concept of productivity is part of a positive *sannyas,* just as the old concept of the nonproductive monk was well adjusted to the negative attitude of *sannyas.*

The positive attitude will have other implications. For example, the old concept of *sannyas* will deny many things. It will deny a family, it will deny sex, it will deny love—it will deny everything that contributes to society's happiness, to your own happiness. It will deny.

I will not deny. That does not mean that I encourage. When

I say that I will not deny, it means only that a moment can come when a person becomes absolutely transcendental to sex; but that is not a requirement, it is a consequence. It is not needed before *sannyas;* it will happen after *sannyas.* And there is nothing to feel guilty about if it does not happen. The old concept that denied love and sex was very cruel. It was both sadistic and masochistic. Sex was denied because sex seems to give a glimpse of happiness.

Many religions have allowed sex without happiness. You can use it for reproduction, but you should not derive any happiness from it. Only then is it not a sin. So sex itself is not really the sin: to be happy is the sin. Sex is allowed if it does not bring you happiness.

To me, nothing that is given to human beings is to be denied or suppressed. Let the inner flowering come first. Then you will see that energy is no longer flowing in the same direction, but then it will happen spontaneously. If energy is no longer moving toward sex, that is something altogether different from denying sex.

If you deny sex, then you have to deny love also. So *sannyasins* who deny sex become loveless. They talk about love, but they become loveless. They talk about universal love. It is always easier to talk about universal love than to love a single individual. To love a single individual is arduous, but to love the whole world is easy; nothing is involved. So one who thinks in terms of denial will talk about universal love and will go on denying and uprooting individual feelings.

Religion that denies sex will have to deny love, because with love there is every possibility that sex may follow. But as I see it, if sex is not denied but is transformed through positive growth— if sex is transformed—then there is no need to deny love. You can be loving. And unless you are loving, the energy that is not being released through the sex center cannot be used. It will become destructive.

To me, a growing love is the only possibility of transcending sex. Love must grow until it includes the whole universe. But it must not begin from there; it can never begin from there. The beginning is always from the near; it is never from the far. One who thinks that he should begin from the far is deceiving himself. You can never begin from far away; every journey has to begin from the near.

The first step that is to be taken cannot be taken from the end. First one should be a loving individual. Then the more one's love grows, the less sexual he becomes and the more the love will spread.

I do not deny anything, because ultimately it is bliss that is being sought. Everyone is seeking bliss. So happiness is not to be denied. Of course, when there is an explosion of bliss, you will know that whatever you have been thinking of as happiness was fake, but you cannot know it now.

Let the bliss come first. That is what I mean by positive growth. First let something come to you, something greater. Only then can the lesser be thrown. And your ego will not be strengthened by it because when you throw it, you are throwing something useless, worthless. Those who talk about renunciation—who say, "I have left this or that"—show by their claims that nothing meaningful has been achieved. Whatever they have renounced still remains meaningful to them. It is there in their memory; it is still part of their mind. It still belongs to them. Of course, they have renounced it, but how can you renounce something that does not belong to you? So if you go on thinking about what you have renounced, it still belongs to you—in a negative way.

Once you know a greater phenomenon, a greater bliss, a greater happiness, then you are not renouncing anything. Things just drop away, like dry leaves from a tree. No one knows about it, no one is doing it: the dry leaves just drop. The tree remains oblivious to it and there is no loss felt.

To me, everything has a moment to happen, a moment of ripeness. Ripeness is everything. One must ripen, otherwise one will be wandering unnecessarily, harassing oneself unnecessarily. One should ripen. Then the opportunity comes by itself. Renunciation should only be through positive growth.

That is what I mean by my *sannyas:* renunciation through

positive growth. It is not negative at all. There is no denial, no suppression. I accept the human being as he is. Of course, much that exists in him is only potential, it is not yet realized; but as man is, he is not to be condemned. There is nothing to be condemned: he is the seed. If you condemn the seed, how can you acclaim the tree?

I accept the human being as he is—totally, with no denial at all. Only I do not say that this is all he can be, that this is the end. I only say that this is the beginning. The human being is only a seed that can grow into a great tree, that can grow into divinity. Each human being can be a god, but now—as he is—he is only a seed. The seed is to be protected, the seed is to be loved, and the seed is to be given every opportunity to grow.

Sannyas means that you have come to realize that you are a seed, a potentiality. This is not the end; this is only the beginning. To be initiated into *sannyas* means that you have decided to begin that growth. The growth comes through freedom; the growth comes through insecurity.

A seed is very secure; a tree is not so secure. The seed is closed; it is closed completely. The moment the seed dies and begins to grow, its potentiality begins to be awakened. But there are dangers: insecurity will be there, there is every possibility of destruction—a very delicate thing is fighting against the whole universe. But if you remain only a seed, there is no danger.

To be a *sannyasin* means that now you take the decision to grow. And this is the last decision. Now you will have to struggle; now you will have to live in insecurity. Now you will have to live with dangers; you will have to fight them and face them moment to moment. This moment-to-moment fight, this struggle, this living in the unknown, is the real renunciation.

To decide to grow is a great renunciation: a renunciation of the security that is given to the seed, a renunciation of the wholeness that is given to the seed. But this security is at a very great cost. The seed is dead; it is only potentially living.

As far as I know, human beings—unless they decide to grow, unless they decide to take a jump into the unknown—are like seeds: dead, closed. To be a *sannyasin* is to make a decision to grow, to make a decision to move into dangerous territory, to make a decision to live in indecision.

This seems paradoxical. It is not. One must begin somewhere. Even to live indecisively must be a decision; even to go into insecurity is going somewhere. One has to decide to do it. I help you to make your decision; I create a situation in which you can make the decision.

This neo-*sannyas* can go to the very core of the world. It can reach everyone because nothing special is needed, only understanding. Another thing I would like to explain is that this *sannyas* is not bound to any religion. Every type of *sannyas* on earth has been part and parcel of a particular religion, a particular sect. This too is a part of our need for security. You renounce, and still you belong. You say, "I have left the society," and yet you belong to a sect. You go on being a Hindu, a Moslem, or a Sikh; you go on being something.

Really, *sannyas* means to be religious and not to be bound to any religion. Again, it is a great jump into the unknown. Religions are known, but religion itself is the unknown. A sect has a system; religion has no system. A sect has scriptures; religion has only the existence, not scriptures.

My *sannyas* is existential, religious, nonsectarian. This does not mean that my *sannyas* will deny a Mohammedan his Mohammedanism, that it will deny a Christian his Christianity, no. It means, really, quite the reverse. It will give a Christian the real Christianity, it will give a Hindu the real Hinduism, because the deeper you go into Christianity or Hinduism, the more you find that Christianity or Hinduism drops and only religiousness is there. The deeper you go into Christianity, the less it will be like Christianity and the more it will be like religiousness.

With *sannyas*, you reach to the very center of religiousness. So when I say that by becoming a *sannyasin* you belong to no religion as such, I do not mean that you are denying Christianity or Hinduism or Jainism. You are only denying the dead part in religion that has become burdensome. You are only denying the dead tradition, and you are uncovering and discovering again the living current—the living current behind all the dead traditions, dead scriptures, dead gurudoms, dead churches.

You are again finding the living current. It is always there; it always has to be rediscovered. Each one has to discover it again. It cannot be transferred; it cannot be transmitted. No one can give you the living current. Whatever has been given will be dead. You will have to dig for it deep within yourself, otherwise you will never find it. So I am not giving you a religion; I am only giving you a push so that you can find the living current. It will be your own finding. It can never be given to you by anyone else. I am not transmitting anything to you.

There is a parable. Buddha came before a crowd one day with a flower in his hand. He was to give a sermon, but he remained silent. Those who had come to listen to him began to wonder what he was doing. Time was passing; this had never happened before. What was he doing?

They wondered whether he was going to speak or not. Then someone asked, "What are you doing? Have you forgotten that we have come to listen to you?"

Buddha said, "I have communicated something. I have communicated something that cannot be communicated through words. Have you heard it or not?"

No one had heard it. But a disciple—a very unknown disciple, known now for the first time—a *bhikkhu* named Mahakashyap laughed, laughed heartily. Buddha said, "Mahakashyap, come here. I give you this flower. All that could be given through words I have given to you all, and that which is really meaningful— which cannot be given through words—I give to Mahakashyap."

Zen tradition has been asking again and again, "What was communicated to Mahakashyap; what was transmitted to Mahakashyap?"—a transmission without words. "What did Buddha say; what did Mahakashyap hear?" And whenever there is someone who knows, he laughs again. The questions are just a trick. When someone understands, he laughs again, but wherever there are persons who are scholars—who know much and at the same time know nothing—they discuss the story. Then they decide what has been heard. But someone who knows will laugh!

Bankei, a great Zen teacher, said, "Buddha said nothing. Mahakashyap heard nothing."

Someone asked him, "Buddha said nothing?"

"Yes," Bankei said. " 'Nothing' was said; 'nothing' was heard. It was said, and it was heard. I am a witness."

So someone said, "You were not there."

Bankei said, "I need not have been there. When 'nothing' was communicated, no one was needed to be a witness. I was not there, and yet I am a witness."

Someone laughed. Bankei said, "He was also a witness!"

The living current cannot be communicated. It is always there; you just have to go to it. It is nearby, just by the corner. It is in you; you are the living current. But you have never looked within; your attention has always been outward. You have been oriented to the outside, and you have become fixated there. Your focus has been so fixed on that outside that you cannot conceive of what it means to be within. Even when you try to be inward, you close your eyes and you continue being outward.

To be *in* means to be in a state of mind where there is no outside and no inside. To be within means that there is no boundary between you and the totality. When there is nothing outside of you, only then do you come to the inner current.

And once you have a glimpse, you are transformed. You know . . . you know something incomprehensible. You know something that the intellect cannot comprehend; you know something that the intellect cannot communicate. Yet one has to communicate —even with a flower, even with a laugh.

It makes no difference how you communicate. These are just gestures. Does it make any difference if I use my lips to speak or if I use my hands to present you with a flower? But if the gesture is new, it disturbs you. When Buddha gave the flower to Mahakashyap it was a gesture, just as when I speak it is a gesture. I make a sound: it is a gesture. I remain silent: it is a gesture. But when the gesture is new, unknown to you, you think that something different is happening. Nothing is different. The living current cannot be communicated, but yet it has to be communicated. Somehow it has to be indicated, somehow it has to be shown.

The moment someone becomes ready to take *sannyas*, it is a decision that he is ready to begin a great search. It is a gesture to me that he is ready to take a jump. And when someone is ready to change—to lose his old identity, to be reborn into a new being —when someone is ready, he need not be qualified. It makes no difference. This readiness *is* the qualification.

When someone is ready, I am ready to push. It is not necessary that he should reach. The wonder is that he should begin.

The beginning is something great. Reaching is not so great as beginning, because whenever someone reaches he is capable and whenever someone begins he is not capable. Do you understand me? Whenever someone reaches he is capable. Whenever someone begins he is incapable. So the beginning is the miracle.

A Buddha is not a miracle. He is capable so he reaches. It is so mathematical, there is no miracle. But when someone comes to me with all his desires, with all his longings, with all his limitations, and thinks to begin, it is a miracle. If I have to choose between Buddha and him, I will choose him. He is a miracle— so incapable and so courageous.

I am not concerned at all with what end you achieve. I am concerned only with the beginning. You begin—and I know that once there is a beginning, the end is half in hand. The beginning is the thing. Once there is a beginning, you will go on growing.

It is not a question of a day or two; it is not a question of time. It may happen the next moment; it may not happen for lifetimes. But once you have begun, you will not be the same again. This very decision to take *sannyas* is such a miracle of change that you will not be the same again. For births and births you may not achieve, but you cannot be the same again.

This same situation will come again; it will recur again. This remembrance of taking a decision to be free will always be there amidst all your slaveries, amidst all your bondages. This decision to be free—this longing to be free, this longing to transcend—will always be there waiting for an opportunity.

So how can I deny anyone a beginning? And whom do I have to ask to know whether someone is qualified or not? If God allows you existence, allows you life, and never asks you, "Are you qualified?" who am I to ask?

I am not giving you life; I am not giving you existence. I am just giving you an opportunity to transform yourself. When God is ready to give you life, with all your limitations and weaknesses, you must be qualified. He allows you to exist; you must be precious. So who am I to deny you a beginning? Sometimes gurus become even wiser than God. They decide who is qualified and who is not. Even if God comes to them, they will decide if he is qualified or not.

Do not laugh! Whenever anyone comes, God is coming. Whenever anyone comes, it is God who is coming because no one else can come. So who am I to deny anyone when he comes to me? He may not know it, he may not be aware of it, but I am aware of it: that God is in search of himself. So I cannot deny anyone; I can just rejoice in each beginning. That is why no distinction is made for my *sannyas,* no qualification is required.

This *sannyas* is needed now for the whole humanity. We have become so unaware of the living current, we have become so unaware of the divinity within and without, that each one has to be made aware.

Otherwise, the situation that exists has become so bad that it may not be possible for humanity to rise again for another century. It has been going on and on like this. Darwin thought that we were animals and now they think that we are automata. At least animals have souls! Or they had; now they don't. Now they think that we are automata. And soon we will not be such efficient automata either, because better computers will be there, better mechanisms will be there. Not only will you be just a machine, but a very ordinary one.

This is a belief; this is not knowledge. But this is the belief that has been forced on the human mind for three centuries. Now it has become a prominent attitude. It is as much a belief as any other belief; it makes no difference whether or not science supports it. It is a belief, and once all of humanity begins to believe it, it will be difficult to revive human souls.

So the days that are coming, the last part of this century, will be very definitive. The latter part of this century will decide the fate of centuries to come. This is going to be a definitive period, definitive in the sense that the belief that human beings are only machines, natural mechanical devices, may become prevalent. If this belief becomes prevalent, it will be very difficult to come again to the living current. It will go on becoming more and more difficult.

Even today it has become difficult. There are so few people in the world who really know the living current. They can be counted on the fingers. All those who talk about it are only talking; very few people really know. And each day the number is falling down without being replaced again. Each day there are fewer and fewer people who know the living current, who know the inner reality, who know consciousness, who know the divine.

This century, the last part of this century, will be decisive. So those who are in any way ready to begin, I will initiate them. If ten thousand are initiated and even one reaches the goal, the trouble is worth taking. And all those who come to know something of this inner world, I would like to ask them to go and knock at every door; I would like to tell them to stand on rooftops and proclaim that something blissful, something immortal, something divine *is.*

Be a witness to it. Go and be a witness to it. Otherwise, the belief that men are mechanical beings will become prevalent. It is easier to put a check on it now; it will not be easy to get rid of it afterward.

And in a way, the human mind is more pliable now than it has ever been, more ready to be molded into any form. Because all the old beliefs have been taken away, the mind is vacant, thirsty to belong anywhere—even to a mechanical belief. Any nonsense which can give you a feeling of belonging, which can give you a feeling that you know what reality is, will be picked up and the human mind will become tethered to it. So not a single moment is to be wasted. Those who know even a little bit, those who have had even a glimpse, should talk about it to others.

The last part of this century is not so short a time as it seems. In a way it is longer than many centuries, because the speed of change is so great. These thirty years will be just like thirty centuries: what could not be done in thirty centuries can be done in thirty years, in three decades. The rapidity of change is such that even a short amount of time is not so short.

There are three beliefs that are going to destroy the last bridge between humanity and the living, divine current. The first is the belief that man is just a mechanism and the mind is just a machine. The second is communism: the belief that man, and man's relationship to society, is just an economic phenomenon. In communism there is no role for the heart. Man is not the deciding factor; economics decides. Man is in the hands of economic forces, blind forces. Then consciousness is not decisive, the social structure is decisive. Marx says that it is not consciousness that determines society, but society that determines consciousness. Then consciousness is nothing. If it is not decisive, it is not.

And third, there is the Freudian concept of irrationality, which says that man is not a rational being at all. Man cannot do anything; man is in the hands of natural forces, instinct. He *has* to do whatever he does. There is no consciousness really: we have only an illusory notion that we are conscious.

There is the Darwinian concept, which has turned into a belief that man is a human machine; the Marxist concept, which has turned consciousness into a epiphenomenon of economic forces; and the Freudian concept of irrationality. These are the three prevalent religions. Neither Mohammedanism, nor Christianity, nor Hinduism, nor Buddhism is a prevalent religion. Neither Buddha, nor Mahavir, nor Mohammed, nor Christ is a prophet now. Today's prophets are Freud, Darwin, and Marx. All three are against freedom and all three are against immortality.

I will go on pushing everyone into the inner world, hoping, of course, hoping against hope, that someone may come to the living current, the *satchitananda,* and may be able to express it through his total being—to live it. If even a few people can be found to live it now, the whole course of future humanity will be changed. But this can happen only through living, not through any teaching. That is why I insist on *sannyas.* It is to help you to begin to live.

I also insist on it in another sense. You may say, "If no outward change is needed, then why do you tell us to change our clothes? Why the change in name?" I want *sannyas* to become infectious. As far as you are concerned, it helps you to remember. For others, the change begins from a point where it gives them something that they can think about. They can be either for it or against it; they cannot be indifferent to it. Your ocher-colored robe—the moment someone sees it, he will be either for it or against it. No one can be indifferent. He will think about it or he will laugh at it. He will either think that you have renounced or that you have gone mad, but in either case he will begin to think about it. And if your ocher robes go on confronting him continuously—if a person is forced to come into contact with these robes so many times daily—it will become infectious. He will not be able to continue neglecting it. He will have to consider it, to decide either for or against it.

I want religion to become a current dialogue. It is not a current dialogue at all; no one talks about it. Everyone talks about politics; no one talks about religion. And if someone talks about it, others only tolerate it out of etiquette; they listen only as a social duty. No one cares today about what is happening to his innermost soul.

Religion has to be made a current topic of conversation, a current dialogue. Every means to do this should be used. A living symbol is needed. Thus, the ocher robes. Wherever you go in your ocher robe you create waves of thinking, waves of emotion. Just passing by, you create a ripple, an atmosphere, a situation. That is why I insist on the change in clothes.

But there are other reasons also. The ocher color helps in so many ways because each color has its own psychology, its own wavelength, its own capacity to absorb. You cannot be the same person in different-colored robes; you will be different. For example, when you are in a white robe, you cannot be the same as when you are in a black robe. In a black robe, you will feel a certain sadness within you, crippling you. Unknowingly, you will become sad. Nothing in this world, in this existence, is meaningless; nothing is insignificant. Everything has a meaning; everything carries a particular atmosphere with it.

A policeman, when he is off duty and not in his uniform, is an ordinary person. You can even see the change in his face, he is so ordinary now. But when he is in his uniform, he is someone else, quite a different person. He is not the same man. His whole behavior will be different: he will stand in a different way, he will walk in a different way. With the change of clothes, he will change. And the attitude of others toward him will change.

The ocher color has been chosen for many reasons. One reason is that it makes you feel just like the sunrise in the morning. It is the color of the sun rising; the rays of the sun in the morning are ocher-colored. The whole atmosphere becomes alive, worth seeing. Everything becomes alive. The color creates a living atmosphere—something alive and vibrating.

So this color was chosen in order that you might vibrate with divinity. You must be alive with divinity; no sadness should have any shelter within you, no sorrow should be allowed to have any shelter. You must be in a dancing mood twenty-four hours. Ocher is a dancing color.

Then, too, always wearing the same color maintains the same atmosphere around your body as in the morning. For the whole day, the same atmosphere is there. If you cooperate with it, you will feel a great difference within yourself.

When one person is wearing ocher it is one thing; when thousands wear it, the result is altogether different. The quantity changes the quality. Buddha would come to a city with ten thousand ocher-colored *bhikkhus* and the whole city would be surrounded by a new atmosphere. It was a great confrontation. That whole day the village would be as fresh as the morning. Everywhere, the ocher color was there; no one could forget it for a moment.

The ocher color has a particular psychological association. For thousands of years it has been associated with *sannyas*. It was used so many times (for thousands and thousands of years it has been used by *sannyasins*), so the association has become part of the collective mind.

You may know that *sannyas* was originally an oriental concept. For at least ten thousand years, *sannyasins* in the Orient have used the ocher color. Throughout many lifetimes you have known the ocher color to be worn by *sannyasins*. It is part of the collective mind, part of the collective unconscious.

The association is very strong, so once you begin to wear ocher the whole past, the collective mind, is revived. Ancient memories come up again and surround you. They change your personality, they change you—they change the inner structure of your mind. It is possible to use another color, but it will be difficult to create the same association with a new color. It will take time, and the time is short now, the moment is crucial. So many have asked me why I chose ocher for my *sannyasins*—why not a new color? A new color can be used, but it will not be helpful now. If I had ten thousand years before me, I would change the color; but now the time is short and decisive and crucial, and a great crisis is to be faced. So I will use your many births. . . .

If you think that whenever someone comes to me I just give him *sannyas*, it is not so. I may say that I will give *sannyas* to anyone who comes, but this does not mean what it seems to mean. It may look as though I just give *sannyas* to anyone, but what is really happening is something quite different.

The moment anyone comes to me, I know much about him that he does not even know about himself. For example, yesterday morning someone came to me and I told her to take *sannyas*. She was bewildered. She said to give her at least two days' time to think about it and decide. I said to her, "Who knows what will happen in two days? So much you require." I insisted, "Take it today, this moment!" but she was not decisive, so I gave her two days.

The following morning, this morning, she came and took *sannyas*. She had not taken two days, only one day. I asked her why. "You have been given two days. Why have you come so soon?"

She said, "At three o'clock at night, suddenly I was awakened. Something deep within me was telling me, 'Go and take *sannyas*.' " It is not a decision that she made, but a decision that has been made by her deep-rooted unconscious.

But the moment she came into the room I knew her, I knew her mind, which she herself came to know twenty-four hours later. So when I say, "Take *sannyas*," there are many reasons. With every person to whom I tell it, the reason will be different. Either he has been a *sannyasin* in his last life, or somewhere in the long journey he has been a *sannyasin*.

I had another name for this *sannyasin* yesterday, but today I had to change it because I gave her that name in her indecision. When she came this morning she herself had decided, so that other name was not needed. Now I am giving her a different name that will be a help to her. I have given her the name Ma Yoga Vivek, because the decision has come through her *vivek*—her awareness, her consciousness.

Ma Yoga Tao is here, for example. She has been a *sannyasin* three times in her past lives. I have given her the name Tao because in a past life she was Chinese and a Taoist monk. She might not be remembering it, but I have given her the name Tao. Someday she will remember her past and then she will know why I have given her a Chinese name. The name is irrelevant now— she is not Chinese—but the moment she remembers that she has been a Taoist monk she will know why the name was given to her.

Everything is meaningful, but it may not be obvious and it may not be possible to explain it to you. Many things will have to remain unexplained for a much longer time. The more receptive you become, the more I will be able to explain. The deeper your capacities to be sympathetic, the deeper the truth that can be revealed.

The more rational the discussion, the less truth that can be revealed. Only truths of small significance can be proved by reason. Deeper truths cannot be proved. So unless I feel that you are so sympathetic that reason will not come in, there are many things that I cannot tell you. I have to remain silent on many points—not because I am withholding anything from you, but because it will not be helpful to you. On the contrary, it may prove harmful.

3

Initiation: Stepping Out of the Wheel of Sansar

Last time you spoke about the mala, *about changing the color of the clothing, about changing the name, and the reasons for these things. Why do you wish your own picture to be worn around the neck—especially when you deny being a guru?*

I deny being a guru, but I do not deny your being a disciple. One should never be a guru, but discipleship is something without which nothing is possible. When there is no guru, then discipleship is something inner—an inner discipline. In fact, both words come from the same root: *discipulus.* It means a mind that is ready to seek, search, learn; a mind that is open and vulnerable. So I deny being a guru, but I do not deny your being a disciple.

Another point: the *mala* with a picture on it has so many reasons behind it. First, the picture is not mine. Had it been mine, I would have hesitated to put it there. No one would be courageous enough to put his own picture there. Everyone will think of doing it, but no one will actually put it there.

The picture only appears to be mine; it is not. No picture of me is possible really. The moment one knows oneself, one knows something that cannot be depicted, described, framed. I exist as an emptiness that cannot be pictured, that cannot be photographed. That is why I could put the picture there.

Two or three more things are to be understood. The more you know the picture—the more you concentrate on it, the more you come in tune with it—the more you will feel what I am saying. The more you concentrate on it, the more there will not be any picture there. But this is something you will have to do in order to know.

In the evening meditations, you are to concentrate on me for forty minutes without closing your eyelids for a single moment. Those who concentrate for forty minutes continuously come to know many times that I am not there. The place where I am becomes empty and vacant. And unless one knows this, he has not been able to concentrate.

So this picture is given to you for meditation. The more you go into meditation, the more you will come to know that the locket is empty. When you concentrate on the locket, you become attuned to me. And only in that moment when there is no picture—when you know that the locket is vacant (that there is no one), when only nothingness is there—can you communicate with me. That is one reason why I have given the locket to you.

Another reason is that you are going to develop in many ways and the more you progress—the more you proceed toward meditation, the more you become meditative—the more you will become sensitive and vulnerable to many different influences, some of which may be harmful to you. Ordinarily you are not so vulnerable, so sensitive, because ordinarily you are not so alive.

With meditation going deeper and deeper, you will be more open to many different influences. Many of them may be harmful to you, and you may have to be protected. This *mala*—this picture, this locket—will protect you. It is a secret science, so I can only indicate something about it. The locket with the picture is only symbolic, but until you become so strong, until you become so deeply transformed that you need no protection, it will help you to continue remembering me. That remembrance will be a help, a protection. With this picture, unknowingly, unconsciously, you will remember me many times during the day. I cannot rely upon you to remember—that is why the picture is needed. You may forget, and the gap may prove harmful.

Once I have given you *sannyas,* once I have become your witness, once I have initiated you, I have become responsible for you in many ways. In a way you have surrendered to me; I must look after you. You cannot always be with me, but I can always be with you. So the locket is to make you remember me, unknowingly. Others will make you remember; anyone who sees you will ask you first about the picture. And the moment you remember me, even unknowingly, I am there. But this you will come to know by and by.

Many reasons are there, but I will not talk about them. This much is enough. Other reasons will be revealed by and by, but it is better that they should not be revealed now. There are things that should not be talked about, because even by talking about them, they become superficial. There are things that should remain occult, secret. They can work only in secrecy; otherwise they won't work. They are just like the roots of a tree. The roots must remain underground, in the dark, unknown to the tree. Only then can they work.

So there are occult things that must remain unconscious, underground. You must not know them. Only then do they work; otherwise they will not work. The roots must not be known, they must remain hidden. So there are many things you may ask that I will not answer. Or I will answer only up to the limit where what is hidden is not uncovered. The hidden must remain hidden. You will come to know it, but only by experience.

After three months you will not be able to remain for a single moment without the *mala.* You will feel the difference. But that will be your knowing. It is so great that it cannot remain unfelt. And by and by, as the experience grows deeper and richer, you will not feel that the picture is there at all. With the deepening of your consciousness, the locket will become empty. Everyone else will see the picture, but not you. When this happens, then you can communicate with me directly, immediately, without any medium.

I am trying in so many ways to convey things without any medium, because there are things that cannot be conveyed through any medium. So I will have to create devices. This *sannyas*, too, is a device; this initiation, too, is a device. Those who are initiated will soon become capable of knowing things that cannot be told to others—of so many secrets, keys, which no one can ordinarily understand unless he has been seasoned, ripened, through occult training.

This is only the beginning. Much is to follow. If I feel you are receptive, then much will follow. If I feel you are not receptive, then the beginning will be the end. You will gain much even through the beginning, but not the whole thing. So in many ways I will try to come to know your receptivity.

If someone comes to me and takes *sannyas*, I give him a *mala* with the picture on it. It is predictable that he should ask, "Why am I to wear this picture of yours?" This question is very predictable. But if he does not ask, if he simply takes the *mala* and asks no questions—if he is not curious—then he has given a deeper hint about himself: things that cannot be questioned can be delivered to him. There are things that cannot be delivered if questioned, because no proof can be given for them, no reasoning can be given for them. There cannot be answers to some questions. They are bare statements of knowing—with no proofs, no criteria. So if someone comes to me and I give him something that the ordinary mind is prone to ask questions about and he does not ask them, he has proved that he is capable of being given deeper things, things that should not be questioned.

How tethered you are to the reasoning part of the mind must be known. I have to know it, because the more you are tethered to reason, the less capable you are of knowing the deeper things. Reason is the most superficial part of your being, the *most* superficial. Although it claims to be the deepest part—only the superficial claims to be the deepest—reason is the most superficial part of your being. It has something to do, it has some utility, but only utility. If you think of it as a vehicle to move into the unknown, then you will never be able to know anything that is worth knowing.

I use many devices to know you. Each and everything I do has many reasons. For example, take the case of someone who resists. Fifteen days ago someone wrote me a letter saying, "I want to be initiated by you, but I cannot make you my guru."

I am no one's guru; I myself never claim to be a guru. But to this man I will claim to be a guru. To this man I cannot say, "I allow you not to think of me as your guru." I cannot say that to this man. He has shown his incapacity so clearly.

If you are not a disciple, then I will have to be a guru. But if you are a disciple, then I need not be a guru; there is no necessity. If you insist on your egoistic nonsurrender, then I will have to insist on many things to destroy your ego. I will have to use many devices to make you egoless.

If you are egoless, then I will not use any device. So the problem becomes more puzzling. To one who is ready to be a disciple, I will say, "I am not your guru. It is enough that you are a disciple." But to one who says, "I cannot believe you. I will not take you as my guru," I will insist. Otherwise this man cannot be initiated. He is coming with a condition, and you cannot be initiated with conditions.

Initiation means that you are ready to surrender, ready to trust. If you are not ready, there is no need to be initiated. This is nothing: this *mala* is nothing; this robe is nothing. This is only the entrance. Now the ways will be darker. There will be things that you have not imagined. You will have to trust; otherwise you cannot proceed a single step. So it is better to know at the entrance that you are incapable of trust, that any effort to lead you further on will be unnecessary and futile.

Religion is basically neither believing nor disbelieving. Religion is trusting. Whenever something unknown is to be jumped into, there is no other way. Unless you trust you cannot move into the unknown. You can only trust and take the jump. The *mala* will also help you to create this trust.

When I say that if you meditate on the picture, the picture will be absent, do not take it on trust. Try it, and it will happen. When I say that when the picture is absent you can communicate with me, do not take it on trust. Try it. Take it hypothetically; experiment with it. The moment the picture is absent and you can communicate with me, you will be ready for the things that will need your trust. Then you can take further steps with a trusting mind.

The more civilization has progressed, the more the ego has become crystallized. The ego is the only barrier. And now it is the greatest barrier. It was not always so.

Sariputra came to Buddha. He was one of the most learned men of those times. He questioned many things; he asked many questions. He discussed many things; then he was initiated. From the moment he was initiated, continuously for thirty years he was with Buddha. But then he would never ask anything.

Someone asked him, "Sariputra, you are such a learned man. People say you know even more than Buddha" (as far as information is concerned, he was a *mahapandit,* a great scholar). "When you came, you discussed such deep things; you questioned many things. We were very happy that someone had come who questioned Buddha in this way so that we could come to know many things that might have remained unknown. Through your questions we could know them. Why have you become silent now?"

Sariputra said, "The moment I was ready to be initiated I had to stop my questions. Now to question anything is absurd. I questioned everything before—before I began to trust. Now my mind is settled."

Sometimes Buddha would say such absurd things just to find out whether Sariputra would question him. He said such absurd things that someone would ask, "What are you saying?" But Sariputra would be silent.

Buddha said to Sariputra, "Wherever you are, always pay respect to the direction in which I am. Wherever you are!" Wherever he was wandering, he would always pay respect in the direction where Buddha was dwelling.

After Buddha's death, Sariputra himself became enlightened. Someone said, "You yourself have become awakened. Now you need not pay respect to anybody. You yourself have become a Buddha."

Sariputra said, "I could not pay respect before because I was not awakened and the ego was there. Now I cannot pay respect because I have become awakened. Then when will I pay respect? I could not pay respect before—and even if I paid respect, it was with great difficulty. But the respect paid with difficulty is no respect. Then I could not pay respect because of the ego and now you say I should not pay respect because I have become awakened. Then when will I pay respect?" Sariputra said, "Buddha does not need it, but now is the moment! Before it was impossible."

But those were times when trust was easy. Now trust has become quite impossible. That is why religion has become impossible.

Religion is bound to be irrational and contradictory; to jump into the unknown is bound to be irrational. It is a jump from the rational to the irrational. By and by, I will have to make you ready and prepared. Little by little, I will make you ready to go into the irrational. Even if I answer your questions it is not to convince your reason, but just to shatter it.

If I appear to be rational sometimes, it is only as a beginning. It is how I begin to work with your mind. If you feel that I am rational, then your mind is attuned. And the moment I see you are attuned, I will push you into the irrational.

There is no other way except to be pushed into the irrational. The more you are ready, the more I will push you into things that will look insane in others' eyes. The moment I see that you are ready to be insane—when you are not afraid of others' eyes and others' opinions, when you are not even afraid of your own irrationality—only then can the deeper keys be handed over to you, not before. Otherwise you will just throw the keys away; you will not be able to appreciate them. You will not even be able to understand them—that they are keys.

So by and by, all those who have been initiated into *sannyas* will have to be ready to go into the irrational. Existence is such!

It does not respond to questions. Life is such. It gives no explanations; it *is*. All our questions and all our answers are only deceptions. Even scientific answers are deceptions because they never really answer anything. They only push the question a step behind. They go on pushing the question further and further back until you become so tired that you stop asking.

No question is answerable through answers. Through an existential jump every question is solved, but not through the intellect. If you ask a scientist why oxygen and hydrogen combine to create water, he will say that it just happens; it is so. "We can only say this much: that it happens." But why does it happen? No one will ask a scientist why oxygen and hydrogen create water and why helium and oxygen can't create water. There is no answer. The scientist will say, "We can only say how it happens, not why."

But with religion, we always ask why. Even science, which claims to be rational, cannot answer why. Yet religion, which never claims to be rational, is always asking why.

You ask me, "Why this *mala*, why this picture?" and I will say, "Use it in this way, and this will happen." My answer is as scientific as possible. If you ask why, even science (which claims to be rational) cannot answer. Religion never claims to be rational. Its only claim is of being irrational.

Use the *mala* in this way: meditate on the picture. Then the picture will not be there. It happens! Then the absent picture becomes a door, and through that door you can communicate with me. It happens so. After meditating, take the *mala* off and feel. Then put the *mala* on and feel, and you will see the difference. Without the *mala* you will feel totally unprotected, in the hands of a force that can be harmful. With the *mala* on, you will feel protected. You will be confident, more settled. Nothing can disturb you from the outside.

This is what happens. If you experiment with it you will come to know. But why it happens cannot be answered scientifically. And from a religious point of view there is no question to answer, because religion never claims.

Many rituals of religion become irrelevant. As time passes, a very meaningful ritual may become meaningless because certain keys are lost and no one can say why the ritual exists. Then it becomes just a dead ritual. You cannot do anything with it. You can perform it, but the key is lost. For example, you can go on wearing the *mala,* but if you do not know that the picture on it is meant for some inner communication, then it will just be a dead weight. Then the key is lost. The *mala* may be with you, but the key is lost. One day you will have to throw away the *mala* because it is useless.

The *mala* is a device for meditation. It is a key. The night meditation, where you gaze at me for forty minutes without blinking, is the key; and one who can move deeply into the night meditation will know the secret door hidden within the locket. But this will happen only through experience. I can only help you toward the experience, but unless it happens to you, you will not know it. It can happen. It is so easy; it is not difficult at all. While I am alive it is easy, but when I am not there it will be very difficult.

All the religious statues that have existed on earth were used as such devices. But now they are meaningless. Buddha declared that his statue should not be made, but the inner work that can happen with a statue still had to be done. The statue itself is meaningless; the real thing is the work that can be done through it. Those who follow Mahavir can communicate with Mahavir through his statue even today, but what about Buddha's disciples?

That is why the bodhi tree became so important. It was used instead of Buddha's statue. For five hundred years after Buddha there was no statue of him. In Buddhist temples only a picture of the bodhi tree and two symbolic footprints were kept. But this was sufficient! The tree that exists in Bodh Gaya is a continuation of the original tree, and those who know the key can communicate with Buddha today through the bodhi tree at Bodh Gaya. It is not meaningless that monks from all over the world come to Bodh Gaya. But they must know the key or they will go there and the whole thing will be just a ritual.

There are keys—particular mantras chanted in a particular way, pronounced in a particular way, emphasized in a particular way with such and such a frequency so that a particular wavelength is created. Then the bodhi tree is not just a bodhi tree. It becomes a passage; it opens a door. Then twenty-five centuries disappear; the time-gap is lost. You come face to face with Buddha. But keys are always lost. . . .

So this much can be said: use the locket and you will know much. All that I have said will be known, and more. That which I have not said will also be known.

What does it mean to be a spiritual seeker?

It means two things primarily. One, that life as it is known outwardly is not fulfilling; life as it is known outwardly is meaningless. The moment one becomes aware of the fact that this whole life is just a meaningless thing, seeking begins. This is the negative part, but unless this negative part is there, the positive cannot follow.

Spiritual seeking primarily means a negative feeling: a feeling that life, as it is, is meaningless. The whole process ends in death: dust unto dust. Nothing remains conclusively in one's hands. You pass through life with such agony, with such hell, and nothing conclusive is achieved.

This is the negative side of spiritual seeking. Life itself helps you toward this. This part—this negativity, this frustration, this anguish—is the part the world is to do. Once you become really aware of the fact of the meaninglessness of life as it exists, then your seeking ordinarily begins, because you cannot be at ease with a meaningless life. With a meaningless life an abyss is created between you and everything that is life. An unbridgeable gap grows, becoming wider and wider. You feel unanchored. Then a search for something meaningful, blissful begins. That is the second part, the positive part.

Spiritual seeking means to come to terms with actual reality, not with a dream projection. Our whole life is just a projection, our dream projection. It is not to know what is; it is to achieve what is desired. You can take the word "desire" as a symbol of our so-called life. Life is a desired projection: you are not in search of what is; you are in search of what is desired. You go on desiring and life goes on being frustrating because it is as it is. It cannot be as you like it. You will be disillusioned. Not that reality is antagonistic to you, but you are not in tune with reality, only with your dreams. Your dreams will have a shattering disillusionment. While you are dreaming it is all right, but when any dream is achieved, everything becomes disillusioning.

Spiritual seeking means knowing this negative part: that desiring is the root cause of frustration. To desire is to create a hell of one's own accord. Desiring is the world: to be worldly is to desire and to go on desiring, never becoming aware that each desire comes to nothing but frustration. Once you become aware of this, then you do not desire. Or, your only desire is to know what is.

Now you decide, "I am not going to project myself, I am going to know what is. It is not that I should be this way, or reality should be that way, but only this: whatever reality may be, I want to know it—naked as it is. I will not project; I will not come in. I want to encounter life as it is."

Positively, spiritual seeking means encountering the existence as it is, without any desire. The moment there is no desire, the projection mechanism is not there working. Then you can see what is. Once known, this "what is"—that which is—gives you everything.

Desires always promise and never give. Desires always promise bliss, ecstasy, but in the end it never comes, and each desire only turns into more desire. Each desire only creates in its place more desires that are still greater and, of course, in the end more frustrating.

A no-desiring mind is one that is engaged in spiritual seeking. A spiritual seeker is one who is completely aware of the nonsense of desire and is ready to know what is. Once one is ready to know what is, reality is always by the corner, just by the corner. But you are never there. You are in your desires, in the future. Reality is always in the present—here and now—and you are never in the present. You are always in the future: in your desires, in your dreams.

In your dreams, in your desires, you are asleep. And the reality is here and now. Once this sleep has been broken—the dream has been broken and you become awakened to the reality that is here and now, in the present—you are reborn. You come to ecstasy, to fulfillment, to all that has always been desired but never achieved.

Spiritual seeking is to be here and now. You can be here and now only when there is no desiring mind. Otherwise, the desiring mind will create a wavering, just like a pendulum. The mind either goes to past memories or to future desires and dreams, but it is never here and now. It always misses the point of here and now. It goes to one extreme or the other—to the past or the future —and you miss the reality between the two.

Reality is here and now. It is never past and never future. It is always present. Now is the only moment, now is the only time; it never passes. Now is eternal. It is always here, but we are not here. To be a spiritual seeker means to be here. You may call it meditation, you may call it yoga, you may call it prayer, but whatever name is given makes no difference. The mind must not exist. And the mind exists only when there is past or future; otherwise there is no mind.

I was talking to someone yesterday. I was telling him that one cannot think in the present. The moment you think, it has become the past. So the mind cannot exist in the present. It exists only in memories of the past and projections of the future. It never comes in contact with the present. It cannot come; that is impossible. So if there are no thoughts, there is no mind.

This no-mindness is meditation. Then you are here and now. Then you explode into reality; then the reality explodes in you.

Spiritual seeking is not to attain *moksha*, salvation. Again, that is a desire, even more greedy than the desire for prestige, for power, for wealth. The desire for *moksha* is even more greedy because it goes even beyond death.

Spiritual seeking is not to seek God, because that again is greed. If you are seeking God, then again your mind is greedy. You must be seeking God *for* something. However deep and unknown to you, however unconscious you are of it, you must be seeking God for something. I do not mean by this that when spiritual seeking comes to a fulfillment there is no God. I am not saying that when meditation happens and the mind is not, *moksha* is not. *Moksha* is there; you are liberated. But it is not a desire. It is a consequence of knowing the reality as it is. God is there, but it is not because of your desiring. He is the reality, so when you know the reality, you know the divine. The reality is divine.

Spiritual seeking is not to seek God or *moksha* or bliss, because, whenever there is desire, you will again project into the future. Spiritual seeking is a disillusionment with the future and a remaining in the present: being in the present, being ready to face whatsoever comes, here and now. The divine explodes, freedom comes, but these are not your objectives. They are shadow consequences of a realization of the real.

First be aware of the whole process of life and its frustrations. Not a single illusion should be there; otherwise, you will be tethered to it. Go deep into each experience of life; do not escape from it. Know it so deeply that you know its disillusionment. Do not escape; do not renounce. Only then can this negative part be complete and can you take a jump into the here and now.

If you have become aware that the future is the root cause of all the nonsense that the human mind creates, then you have taken the basic step. You have traveled. Now you can be ready to be aware of what is. In the first part, the negative part, life helps much. So move deeply into every experience, into every desire, and know it completely. Never renounce prematurely.

This happens. You are not really frustrated with life, but you become greedy for religious promises. You have not known that life is divine, but you have become enchanted with religious heavens. Then everything will be difficult. Because you have not gone through the first part, the second part will be very difficult.

Go through the first part first, and the second part will be easy. The second is difficult only when the first has not been traveled completely. Then you ask how to meditate, then you say that the mind goes on working, then you say that the thought process is continuing. Thoughts cannot be stopped—how can they be stopped? If desire is still there, desire will go on creating thoughts. The first part has not been fulfilled.

A mature spiritual seeker is one who has gone into life without any fear and knows every nook and corner. He has known so much that nothing remains unknown. Then meditation is easy because there is no one to create thoughts, there is no one to create desires. Just by crying, "Hoo!" you can move into the present. Any simple device will make you still. The staff of the Zen masters is just before you: their staff is raised, and you are in the present. Even such a simple device can help if the first part has been fulfilled.

One day the Zen monk Rinzai was speaking in a temple. He had started a sermon, but someone was disturbing him. Rinzai stopped and asked, "What is the matter?"

The man stood up and said, "What is the soul?" Rinzai took his staff in his hand and asked the other people to make way for him. The man began to tremble. He had never expected that this would be the answer.

Rinzai came to him, took hold of his neck with both hands, and pressed it. He kept on pressing and he asked the man, "Who are you? Close your eyes!" The man closed his eyes. Rinzai went on asking, "Who are you?"

The man opened his eyes, laughed, and bowed down to Rinzai. He said, "You have really answered the question 'What is the soul?' "

Such a simple device! But the man was ready. Someone asked Rinzai, "Would you do the same thing to anybody who asked you this question?"

Rinzai said, "The man was ready. He was not asking just for the question's sake. He was ready! The first part was fulfilled. He was really asking; this was a life-and-death question to him. He asked, 'What is the soul?' The first part was fulfilled completely: he was completely disillusioned about life. He was asking, 'What is the soul?' because this life has proved to be a death to him. Now he is asking what life is. No answer from me would have been meaningful. I just helped him to stand still in the present."

Of course, when someone presses your neck, when he is just on the verge of killing you, you cannot be in the future, you cannot be in the past. You will be here and now. If you are not in the moment, it will be dangerous.

If you can say to such a man, "Go deep within and know who you are," the man can become transformed. He can go into *samadhi*. If you can be completely still, completely in the moment—if you can be in the present for even a single moment—you have known reality, you have encountered it, and you will never be able to lose track of it again.

Spiritual feeling is to know what is. What is all this? *This!*—that which is happening right now. What is all this: my speaking, your hearing, this whole thing? What is this? Just stand: be deep in it. Let it come to you and let yourself be open to it.

Then there is a meeting. That meeting is the seeking; that meeting is the whole search. That is what we have called yoga. "Yoga" means "meeting." The very word "yoga" means "meeting": joining again, becoming one once more.

So-called spiritual seekers are not seeking any spirituality. They are only projecting their desires onto a new dimension. But no desire can be projected in the spiritual dimension, because the spiritual dimension is open only to those who are not desiring. Those who desire just go on creating new illusions, new dreams.

First, realize that desire goes on and on, reaching nowhere. Then stand still, and know what desire is. Everything is open; only our desires close us in. The whole existence is open, all doors are open, but we are running with such speed that we cannot see. And the more frustrated we become, the more we increase the speed.

The mind says that you are not running fast enough. That is

why you are not reaching. The mind will not say that *because* you are running you will not reach. How can it say it? It is illogical. The mind says that because you are not running fast enough you are not reaching. So run faster! And those who are running faster are saying the same thing: "Run faster. Those who are running even faster are reaching."

No one is reaching, but there is always someone ahead of you and someone behind you. You have gone ahead of someone, but wherever you are, someone else is always ahead of you. Why?— because desire runs in a circle. We are running in a circle, so if you run very fast, even the person who was behind you may come to be ahead of you. Because we are running in a circle, someone is always going to be ahead and then there will be the feeling that you are not running fast enough—that someone else is reaching and you are losing.

In India we have known many truths. We call this world *sansar. Sansar* means "the wheel." Not only are you running, but the wheel itself is also running. It is not a steady circle: even if you stand still, the wheel will go on. So one does not only have to stop running; one has to step out of the wheel.

This stepping out of the wheel is *sannyas.* Stopping is not enough. You must step off the wheel completely, because even if you are not running, the wheel will go on rotating. It is such a tremendous wheel, with so much force, that you will be moving even if you stand still. *Sannyas* means to step off—not only to stop running, but to step off. Do not be on the wheel at all. Come out of it altogether; be a witness to it. Only then will you know what this wheel is made of and why it goes on running even when *you* are not running.

The wheel is created by infinite desires—by all the desires that have ever existed, all the desires that are in existence today; all the desires of all persons, of all beings, who have ever existed. You will die, but your desires have created waves that will go on. You will not be here, but your desires have created ripples in a new sphere.

It is just like the words I have spoken. You may not be here, but these words, these sounds, will go on vibrating infinitely.

Whatever you have desired, whether it has been fulfilled or un-fulfilled makes no difference. The moment the desire has come into your mind, into your heart, you have created ripples, waves. They will go on and on.

This wheel, this *sansar,* consists of all the desires that have ever existed, all the desires that are in existence. This is such a great force—of all the dead and of all the living—that you cannot stand still. The force will push you; you will have to run.

It is just like being in a crowd. When the whole crowd is running, you cannot stand still. You are pushed to run. You are safe if you are running. If you are not running, you will be killed. Your energy is not needed to run. Even if you do not make any effort, the crowd will push you.

This is the wheel, the wheel of desires. You must have seen the Tibetan picture of the wheel. It is beautifully depicted, the whole wheel of desires.

To step out of the wheel is *sannyas.* You just come out of the crowd; you just step down. You just sit by the side of the road; you say good-bye. Only then do you know the phenomenon: that it is a wheel. Then you know that people are running in a circle: they will pass before you so many times. Then you know that it is a wheel.

A Buddha, a Mahavir, could call this world *sansar,* a wheel, be-cause they knew when they stepped out of it that it was a wheel. It is not that you are running in a straight line. It is a circle. You are repeating the same desires. The same days, the same nights, the same disillusionments go on and on in a whirlwind. Pushed from behind, pulled from the front, you go on. *Sannyas* means to step aside, to step out of the wheel.

This is the second part of *sannyas. Sannyas* has two parts. The first part is knowing the frustration, knowing the anguish. And this is the miracle: once you know that the world is an-guish, frustration, you are not frustrated at all. Frustration comes only because you think the world is *not* frustrating. The anguish comes because you hope, even when you know it is hopeless. That hoping is nonsense. When you know this, then you do not feel hopeless at all. Then there is no need to feel so. Then there is nothing to feel hopeless about—there is no hope.

That is why Buddhism could not be understood. The Western mind could only interpret it as pessimism. It was a natural fallacy. Buddhism is not pessimistic, but to the Western mind it appeared pessimistic because of the saying that the world is frustrating, the world is *dukkha,* misery. This would seem to make you pessimistic.

But this is not the case. The earth has not known so happy, so blissful a person as Buddha. Or, it has known very few such people. Buddha was not a pessimist at all. Then what is the secret? The secret is this: if you know the world is *dukkha,* then you do not expect anything except *dukkha.* Expectation only creates pessimism. Now there is no expectation: you know *dukkha* is the reality. Then there is no need to be in misery.

Once life is known as miserable, you will never be in misery. You will be out of it. So a *sannyasin* is not one who is frustrated. A *sannyasin* is one who has known the world as frustrating. He is not frustrated; he is at ease. There is nothing to frustrate him. Everything that happens—he knows it happens like this. Even death is not an anguish to him, because death is a certainty.

Once you know the nature of this whirling wheel—of this world, of this so-called life, of this repetitive vicious circle—then you will become a silent and a blissful person. Now you do not expect anything, so there is no frustration. Now you do not hope, so there is no feeling of hopelessness. You are at ease, composed. The more you are in the moment, the more you are nonwavering, standing still.

In this very moment, here and now, is all that is to be known and realized: *moksha,* God, the reality. In this very moment! So in a way, spiritual seeking is not for something; it is not for some object. It is to know what is. And the knowing comes once you are in the moment. To be in the moment is the secret door. Or, you may say, the open secret. To be in the moment is the open secret!

4

To Be Intimate with the Divine

Bhagwan, qualities of love and grace have been attributed to the divine. Do these qualities exist? Does the divine exist?

To say that the divine exists will not be right because all that exists is divine. In fact, each and every thing can be said to exist; only the divine cannot be said to exist. Existence itself is divine: to be divine and to exist is to say the same thing in two different ways. So the quality of existence cannot be attributed to the divine.

Everything else can be said to exist because it can go into nonexistence. I can be said to exist because I will go into nonexistence. You can be said to exist because there were times when you were not in existence. But the divine cannot be said to exist because the divine is always there. The nonexistence of the divine is inconceivable. So existence cannot be attributed to the divine. I can only say that existence is divine, or divineness means existence.

Nothing exists that is not divine. You may know it or you may not know it; it makes no difference as far as your divinity is concerned. If you know it, then you become the existence, you become bliss. If you do not know it, you continue in your agony —but still you are divine. If you are asleep, if you are ignorant, then too you are divine. Even a stone is divine—unknown to itself.

Existence is divine. All those who try to prove that God exists do not know. It is sheer nonsense to prove that God exists. And those who try to prove that God does not exist are in the same boat. But no one will try to prove that existence exists. If you say it this way—if you ask me whether existence exists—the question will be absurd.

To me, when someone says that God exists, it means the same thing: existence exists. God and existence are equivalent, synonyms. Once you have become aware of what existence is, you will not call it existence. Then you will call it God. The moment you become aware of the total existence, you cannot use the word "existence." You become more intimate with it so you have to use a personal name. You call it "God." To call existence "God" only means this and nothing else: you can be in an intimate relationship with it.

To call existence "God" means that you can be in personal contact with it. It is not something dead; it is not something to which you cannot be related; it is not something that is indifferent to you. When we say existence is God, we mean to say that existence is intimately related to us, that it is not indifferent to us. So as far as the human mind is concerned, there is not a more accurate word to use for the existence than "God."

But if you ask an orthodox Jew, he will not use the full word "God." He will only use "G-D"; the O is dropped. Orthodox Jews do not use the full term "God"; they use only "G-D." If you ask them why they use "G-D," why the O is dropped, they say: "Whatever we can say is always less than what is. The O is dropped just to symbolize that we are using a word that cannot convey the whole, that cannot be totally comprehensive." The O is symbolic of zero, symbolic of perfection, symbolic of the totality, the whole, so it is dropped and only "G-D" remains.

No word is really meaningful, no word can be comprehensive of the whole. It just indicates something—not something about the divine, but something about the human mind. If you simply say "existence," you are using a term that is neutral. Then you can be indifferent to it and the existence can be indifferent to you. When you use the word "existence" there cannot be a dialogue between you and the existence. Then there is no bridge. But those who have known the existence know that there is a dialogue happening with everything that exists. You can be in an intimate relationship with the existence; you can be in love with it. This possibility of dialogue, of relationship, of being in love, makes the term "God" more meaningful than "existence," but they mean the same.

So I will not say that the divine exists; I will say that all that exists is divine. Existence is divine; to exist is to be divine. Nothing *is* that is not divine. Nothing can be that is not divine. We may know it, we may not know it; we may be aware of it, we may not be aware of it. It makes no difference.

Another thing you asked is whether the qualities of love and grace can be attributed to the divine. Again, no qualities can be attributed to Him because qualities can be attributed to something or someone only if the contrary is possible. Otherwise they cannot be attributed. You can say someone loves you because that someone is capable of not loving you. If he is incapable of not loving you, you will never say he loves you. Then to say it carries no meaning. If I do not love you, I may hate you. Then to say, "I love you," is meaningful. But if I am incapable of hating, then the quality of love cannot be attributed to me. Then love is not a quality, but my very nature.

What is the difference between a quality and one's nature? A quality is something that can be observed in its manifestation but that can also be nonmanifested. A quality is something of which you can be deprived. You can exist without the quality. It is not your intrinsic existence. It is something attributed to you, added to you. It is not your nature.

Nature is something without which you cannot exist. So when someone says, "God is loving," he is not saying exactly the right thing. Jesus is more right when he says, "God is love." Love is His nature, not a quality He possesses. It cannot be replaced. God can be love—love can be God—because love is the intrinsic nature of the divine.

Love is not something added to the divine; it cannot be. It is not possible to conceive of God without love. If you conceive of God without love, you are conceiving of a god who is not a god. To conceive of God without love is to conceive of a god without godliness, because the moment love is erased there is no godliness left behind. So again, I will not say that love is an attribute. Neither will I say that grace is an attribute. They are the very nature of the divine.

Aesop has told us in a fable that a scorpion requested of a turtle by a riverside, "Please carry me to the other shore on your back."

The turtle said, "Do not be foolish. Do not think me to be so stupid. You may sting me in the middle of the stream, and I will drown and die."

The scorpion said, "I am not foolish. Rather, you are foolish because you do not know simple logic. I belong to the Aristotelian school. I am a logician. I will teach you a simple lesson in logic, a simple solution. If I sting you, and if you drown and die, I will also die with you. So be sensible, be logical. I will not sting you. I cannot sting you."

The turtle thought for a moment and then said, "Okay. It seems sensible. Hop on me and off we go."

Exactly in midstream, the sting came. They both were sinking. Before the turtle died it asked, "Where has your logic gone? You have done a very illogical thing. You yourself said that it is simple logic, that you would never do it—and now you have done it. Tell me what happened. Before I die, let me learn another lesson of your logic."

The scorpion said, "This is not a question of logic at all. This is just my character, my nature. I cannot be without it. I can talk about it, but I cannot be without it. I am incapable of being without it really."

Something that you are incapable of doing or not doing indicates your nature. We cannot conceive of the divine as being nonloving or without grace. The love is always there; the grace is always there. We use two words—love and grace—because of our linguistic limitations. Otherwise one word will do. You can call it either "love" or "grace."

We use two words because with love we always expect something in return, but not with grace. Whenever we love someone, something is expected in return. It is always a bargain, however subtle. Told or not told, made known or not made known, it is an inner bargain. Something is expected in return. That is why we use two words: love and grace. With grace, nothing is expected in return. And God never expects anything in return from us.

But as far as divine existence is concerned, love and grace are both one and the same. God is loving—that is His grace. His grace is always with Him. That means He is loving. But those are not qualities that can be attributed to Him. This is His nature. He cannot be otherwise.

We make a distinction between love and grace. We say that someone is known to have received grace or that someone has become the beloved of the divine. This again is a fallacious statement. God is always grace and always love, but we are not always in a receptive mood. Unless we become receptive, we cannot receive it.

When you are not receiving divine grace, it is not that anything is lacking on the part of the divine. There is some kind of barrier within you. You are not receptive to it, you are not open to it, you are not vulnerable to it.

God's nature is grace. But as far as we are concerned, receptivity is not our nature. By nature we are aggressive. We are aggressive—and if the mind is aggressive, it cannot be receptive.

Only a nonaggressive mind can be receptive, so all qualities that carry any type of aggressiveness within them should be dropped. One has to be a door, open to receive—just like a womb. One has to be a total receptivity. Then grace is always flowing and love is always flowing. From everywhere, grace is flowing. Every moment, everywhere, grace is flowing. It is the nature of existence.

But we are not receptive; that is the nature of the mind. Mind is aggressive. That is why I always insist that meditation means no-mind; meditation means a nonaggressive receptivity, an openness.

Logic can never be receptive. Logic is aggressive: you are doing something. Then you cannot be receptive. You can be receptive only when you are not doing. When you are in a nondoing state, absolutely nondoing, simply existing, then you are open from all sides, and from everywhere comes the flow of grace. It is always coming, but our doors are closed. We are always escaping from the grace. Even if it knocks on our doors, we escape.

There is a reason why we go on escaping. The moment the mind is born, it is always safeguarding itself. Our whole training, our whole education, the whole culture of mankind is always so. Our whole mind, our whole culture is based on aggression, competition, conflict. We have not yet become so mature as to learn the secret of cooperation: that the world exists in cooperativeness, not in conflict; that the other, the neighbor, is not just a competitor but a complementary existence that makes me richer. Without him, I will be less. If even a single individual in the world dies, I become a bit less. The richness that was created by him, the richness carried into the atmosphere by him, is no more. Somewhere, something has become vacant.

We live in coexistence, not in conflict, but the training of the mind, of the collective unconscious, always makes you think in terms of conflict. Whenever someone is there, the enemy is there: the enemy is the basic assumption. You can develop a friendship, but it will be developed; the basic assumption is that the other is an enemy.

Friendship can be added to the original feeling, but since the base is inimical—the initial assumption is that the other is an enemy—you can never relax. That is why you can never rely on your friendships. Underneath the friendship, the enemy is there. You have only developed a false friendship; you have added something artificially. Underneath you always know that the enemy is there, the other is the enemy. So even with a friend you are not at ease, even with your lover you are not at ease. Whenever someone else is there you are tense: the enemy is there. Of course, the tension becomes less if you have created a façade of friendship. It is less, but it is there.

There are reasons why this attitude has developed, evolutionary reasons. Man comes from the jungle. His evolution has gone through many stages, many animal stages. Even physiologically the memory remains because the body does not belong to you alone. When I say *my* body, I am claiming something that cannot be claimed. My body has come to me through centuries of development. The basic cell in me is inherited; in my basic cell I have inherited all that has existed before me. All the animals, all the trees—everything that has existed before me has contributed to my basic cell. Within my basic cell is accumulated the whole prior experience of conflict, struggle, violence, aggression. Each cell carries within it the whole evolutionary struggle that has preceded.

Physiologically this is so and mentally also. Your mind has not evolved just in this life. It has come to you through a long journey. The journey may be even longer than the journey of the body itself, because the body has evolved only on earth. It cannot be more than forty million years old; it cannot be older than the earth itself. But the first mind came from another planet, so mind has even deeper evolutionary experiences than the body.

All these experiences make you violent and aggressive. One has to be aware of this total phenomenon. Unless one is aware, one cannot be free from his own past. The whole problem is that one has to be free from his past, and this past is something very great, incomprehensibly great.

All that has lived is still living within you. All that has been is still inside you in seed form, as a potentiality. You come from the past, you are the past, and this past-oriented mind goes on creating aggression, goes on thinking in terms of aggression.

So when religion says to be receptive, the advice remains unheard. The mind cannot think of how it can be receptive. Mind has known only one thing in which it has been receptive, only one thing that it has not been able to do anything about, and that is death. The only thing that the mind has known in which it has had to be receptive is death, so whenever someone says to be receptive, somewhere in the shadows you feel death. If I say to be receptive, the mind will tell you that if you are receptive you will die. "Be aggressive if you want to exist and survive! The fittest survives, the most aggressive one survives. If you are just receptive you will die."

That is why receptivity is never understood—not heard, not understood. Receptivity has been spoken about in many ways. When someone says, "Surrender!" it means be receptive. Surrender means do not be aggressive. When someone says, "Be faithful!" it means be receptive. Do not use logic to be aggressive. Receive the existence as it is; let it come in.

The mind cannot love, because love means to be receptive to someone. Even in love we are aggressive. If you ask Freud he will say that love is nothing but a sort of violence—a mutual violence in which two partners have agreed to become involved. And when Freud says this, he is not just talking nonsense. He means it; he knows something.

Whenever you are in the sex act, whenever you are in intimate love, your behavior is just like fighting. You are fighting. If you go deeply into any act that is the manifestation of what we call love—if you go deeply into it—you will find animal roots. Kissing can become biting at any time. If you go on kissing, if it goes deep, it will be biting. It is just a mild form of biting. Sometimes lovers even say, "I want to eat you." They mean it to be a very loving expression. And in a way, they really try. Sometimes sex goes so deep, becomes so intense, that it is just like a fight.

That is why two partners, two sexual partners, will always alternate between loving and fighting. In the early evening they are fighting, in the night they are loving; in the morning they are fighting, in the early evening they are loving; later on in the night they are fighting. The circle goes on, fighting and loving, fighting and loving. If you ask D. H. Lawrence he will say, "If you cannot fight with your lover, you cannot love." The fight makes it intense, creates an intense situation.

The human mind as it is—as it has evolved out of the past—

cannot love because it cannot be receptive. It can only be aggressive. It is not that you are loving: your love is just a demand for love from the other. Even if you act loving it is just to force the demand. There is a cunning logic. You are always demanding love and if you give love, it is only to make your demand more forceful.

The human mind cannot love. If you ask those who know, those who have really loved—if you ask Buddha, he will say, "Unless the mind dies, love cannot be born." And unless there is love you cannot feel grace, because only in love do you become open.

You cannot love just one particular individual, because it is impossible to be open to a particular individual and closed to all. It is very difficult; it is one of the most impossible things to do; it is not possible at all. If I say that I love you and only you, it is just like saying that whenever you are beside me I breathe, otherwise I do not breathe. If this were the case, then the next time you came to me you would find me dead. Breathing is not something that I can do or not do. Nor is love. But that which is known to us as "love" is like that.

That is why, sooner or later, a lover will find that the other's love has gone dead. And both will know it, both will know that there is no love now. The more lovers know each other, the more unfortunate the situation is. The more they become acquainted with each other, the less hope there is and the more disillusionment. They know that love has gone dead. The love is so narrow, it is forced to be so narrow, that it cannot remain alive.

One has to be loving, not a lover. One has to be loving! This loving must come as an intense, natural manifestation of your being, not as something added to you as an attribute, as a quality. It must be an inner flowering, not a perfume that comes from without. This love is not something you can do. It can happen. It is a happening.

One has to be aware of one's total past. The moment you are aware of your total past, that very moment you have transcended it, you are beyond it, because that which is aware is not the mind.

That which becomes aware of the mind is the consciousness. It carries no past with it. It is eternal. It is always in the now—always new, always here and now.

Consciousness is known only when you become aware of your mind. Then you are not identified with your mind; there is a gap between you and your mind. You know that this is the mind; that this aggressiveness, this hatred, this whole hell, is the mind.

The mind goes on continuously. It will continue to go on and on until you become aware. And this is the miracle: the moment you become aware, the continuity is broken. Now you will be, but not as part of the past. Now you will be of the moment—fresh, young, new. Then each moment you will die, and you will be reborn.

St. Augustine says, "I die every moment." One who has become aware of his whole mind—the whole process of it, the continuity, the continuation of the past that forces itself into the future—one who has become aware of this will die each moment. Each moment the past will be thrown out. One will be fresh, new and young, ready to jump into the new moment that is coming.

Only this fresh consciousness, this eternally young consciousness, is receptive, open. There are no walls to it, no boundaries to it. It is completely open, like an unbound, open space. The Upanishads call it "the inner space of the heart." There is space, simply space. This is consciousness, *sakshi*—the manifestation of awareness.

This transcendence of the mind, of the past, makes you open and vulnerable from all sides, makes you open in all dimensions. Then grace falls on you from everywhere: from the trees, from the sky, from human beings, from animals, from everywhere. Even a dead stone is filled with grace. You feel grace falling on you from everywhere.

Then you do not call it simply existence, you call it God. This metamorphosis, this transformation of your own mind, this transformation of the dead mind into an eternally living consciousness —from the junk of the mind to the open sky of consciousness— this transformation changes your attitude toward existence. Then the whole existence is just a flow of love—friendly, compassionate, loving, graceful. Then you are loved through thousands of hands.

The Hindu religion has created deities with a thousand hands. It means that from everywhere the hand of the divine is there. There is nowhere you can go where the divine hand will not be upon you; everywhere it embraces you. You can go anywhere. Now there is nowhere where the divine is not.

Nanak went to Kaba. He was tired. When he reached the mosque he put down his small bundle of whatever it was and went to sleep. The priest was furious because his legs were facing the holy stone. He pulled Nanak around and said to him, "What foolishness are you doing here? Do you not even know this much respect: that your legs should not be toward the holy stone? Are you an atheist or something?"

Nanak's sleep was broken. He sat up and said, "Then put my legs in the direction where God is not, and do not disturb me."

There is no direction where God is not because every direction is divine: existence itself is divine. But you must be open to it. The whole tragedy, the whole dilemma of the human mind, is that the mind is closed. The mind is an enclosure, but it goes on searching for that which will be freedom. The mind is an imprisonment, and this imprisonment goes on seeking freedom. This is the whole tragedy of human existence.

Mind is a prison. It cannot find freedom anywhere. It must die before freedom can come. But we have taken the mind to be us; we are identified with it. We never think that the death of the mind will be a freedom for us.

Mind is something other than you, but you go on being identified with the mind. How can you come out of the past if you have become identified with the past? The one who has forgotten that he is a prisoner is the most imprisoned because then there is no possibility of freedom. A prisoner can become aware of his imprisonment, but if you are identified with your imprisonment it is impossible. Your body is the boundary of the imprisonment; your mind is the imprisonment itself.

Be aware, be conscious of your mind. And you *can* be conscious of it because you are something different from it. The dream can be broken because you are not the dream. The dream is happening to you, but you are not the dream. You can shatter this imprisonment and come out of it because you are not the imprisonment. The problem is there because you have such a long association with the body and the mind.

Understand this well: that your body is new to you—each birth is new, each beginning is new—but the mind is old. It is a continuation from your previous births, your past births. That is why if someone says your body is ill you are never angry. You feel that he is sympathetic to you. But if someone says your mind is mad, your mind is ill, you are mentally deranged, then you become angry. Then you do not feel he is sympathetic to you. He does not seem friendly.

The association with the body is only an association of this birth. You have been associated with other bodies that have died. The association with the body is broken with each death. It has been broken so many times that even someone who thinks of himself as the body is not as identified with the body as with the mind. If his body falls ill, if there is something wrong with it, he doesn't feel that there is something wrong with *him*.

I was reading about an alcoholic. He was sentenced many times; for the tenth time the same judge was sending him to jail. The judge said, "It is only alcohol, alcohol, alcohol that is the root cause of your problems."

The man said, "Thank you, sir. You are the only person who has not made me responsible. Everyone else says I am at fault. You are the only man who understands me. Alcohol is at fault. I am not responsible at all."

If there is something wrong with the body, you do not feel you are responsible, but if there is something wrong with the mind, you feel that you are responsible. The identification is deeper. It has to be so because the body is the outer layer of your being and the mind is the inner layer. It is the inner you. You can be more identified with it; it has been with you for so many lives. The mind is the old, always the old—it is your continuity—but you are not the mind.

This can be known, there is no difficulty in knowing it. Just be a witness: whenever the mind is working, just sit aside and watch how it works. Do not interfere; do not come in. Coming in will strengthen the mind and you will be identified with it again, so do not come in, do not say anything, do not be a judge. Sit aside as if the traffic is passing on the road and you are just sitting by the side of the road watching it. Do not make any judgments. If you can sit aside even for a single moment and look at the traffic of the mind, the continuous traffic, you will see the gap, the gap between you and the mind. Then the gap can be made greater, wider—unbridgeable.

Finally, the gap between you and the mind becomes so great that there is no bridge between the two. When you have seen from all possible points that the mind is somewhere and you are somewhere else—that you are always inside, always somewhere else—when this is not a theory but a realized fact, a realization, then you are open. Then you have jumped into an inner space, into the inner sky, into the inner space of the heart. You have jumped in. Now you are there, and you are open.

You will know, then, that you have always been open. You have been sleeping in an open sky, but dreaming that you are in prison. Thoughts are nothing but the substance that dreams are made of; they are of the same stuff. In the day you call them thoughts and at night you call them dreams. But because your thoughts are more transparent than your dreams, it is easier to become identified with them.

Anything that is transparent is easy to miss. If there is a totally transparent glass between you and me, I will forget that the glass is there. I will think that I am seeing you directly. This means that I have become so totally identified with the glass that I do not know it is there. My eyes and the glass have become one.

Thoughts are transparent, more transparent than any glass you can look through. They are not at all a hindrance to you. That is why the identification with them is so deep. The transparency of thoughts is so close to you that you forget totally that there exists a mind which is always around you, always between you and the world. Between you and your lover, between you and your friend, between you and your God—wherever you are, it is always there.

Wherever you go, your mind is always a step ahead of you. It is not only that it follows you like a shadow; it is always one step ahead of you, it has reached before you. But you are never aware of it because it is so transparent. Whenever you enter a temple, your mind has entered before you. When you go to a friend, when you are embracing him, your mind has already embraced him. You can see this for yourself and know it.

Your mind is always rehearsing. This stepping ahead is a rehearsal. Before you speak, the mind always rehearses what to say; before you act, it is always rehearsing how to act. Before you do anything or do not do anything, it is rehearsing; the rehearsal is constantly going on. The rehearsal means that the mind is preparing itself; it is one step ahead of you.

This creates a constant, transparent barrier between you and everything else that you come across, that you encounter. No encounter can be real, authentic, because something else is always standing between. You can neither love nor pray, you cannot do anything that requires the removal of the barrier.

Grace is not felt because the barrier is always there, surrounding you like a transparent shell. Neither grace nor love are God's attributes—they are the very nature of the divine—but we are not open to them. When someone is open, he becomes a receiver.

Even then it is not right to say that he has received grace, because now nothing exists except God, nothing exists except grace. Once the barrier is no longer there, nothing exists except God. There is nothing left for the ego to stand upon. One cannot say, "I" so he cannot say, "I have become capable of receiving grace." He can only say, "I have received grace because I was not there." "I" was the barrier. Once "I" is not, he can only say, "It is due to God's grace. What can I do? I am no more."

He is right when he says he has received grace, but when we

say he has received grace we are not right. We are only deceiving ourselves. We are deceiving ourselves because we are not recognizing a great transformation in him. The ego will not let us recognize it. The ego will say, "God is bestowing grace upon him and not upon me." Then we create this very misguided notion: that God can give grace to someone.

He *is* grace. If someone is ready to receive it, He is always giving. It is not even that when someone is ready to receive, He is ready to give. He is always giving. Even when you are not ready to receive, then too He is giving. When you are closed, then too He is raining, His blessings are raining. Be open, and you will know it.

Be conscious, and be open. Only then can you know what love is, what grace is, what compassion is. They are one and the same thing; they are not different things. Basically they are one and the same.

Only then can you know what prayer is. When the barrier is not there, the mind is not there, then prayer is not to ask for something. It is not begging; it is a thanksgiving. Whenever prayer is a begging for something, the barrier is there. The begging is the barrier, the mind is the barrier.

Whenever prayer is a thanksgiving—not for something, but a thanksgiving for all that is. . . .Whenever grace is received, you feel gratitude. From your side there is gratitude; from God's side there is grace.

On the receiver's end, gratitude is felt. We have not known gratitude at all; we cannot know it until we have known grace. We cannot feel gratitude unless we have felt the grace of the divine. But it can be known, it can be felt.

Do not begin such a search; do not begin to inquire about the divine. It is metaphysical and useless. This has been going on for centuries: philosophers have been thinking about what the attributes of God are. There have been metaphysicians who will say that this is the attribute of God and that is not. Someone will say He has no attributes—*nirguna*—and someone else will say He is all attributes—*saguna.* But how can we know that which we haven't known ourselves? How can we decide whether God has attributes or no attributes, whether He is loving or not? Just by thinking about it we are not going to decide. That is not possible.

Metaphysics can only lead us into absurdity. When the human imagination proceeds logically, we think that we have achieved something, but we have not achieved anything. The imagination is ours—we have not known anything beyond ourselves.

Always begin with yourself if you are to escape from metaphysics. And if you cannot escape from metaphysics you cannot be religious. Metaphysics and religion are opposite poles. Do not begin with God at all; always begin with your mind. Where you are—always begin from there. If you begin from your mind, then something can be done. Then you can know something. Then something can be transformed; then it is within your capacity to do something.

If you use your capacity to do something with yourself to the fullest, you will grow, you will expand. The barrier will be gone; your consciousness will be naked. Only then will you begin to be in contact with the divine. And once you have begun to be in contact with the divine, you know what grace is, what gratitude is.

Grace is what you feel showering upon you from everywhere, and gratitude is what you feel within your heart, at the center of that inner space upon which the whole is showering its love, its compassion, its grace. Only then is it meaningful to say, "God" or "Hare Ram." Otherwise our words are just words—not known from existence, but only learned from language, from scriptures.

So I will not say what the attributes of God are. As far as I am concerned, as far as I know, God has no attributes. This does not mean that when we come in contact with Him we will not feel His love, His grace. It only means that these are not His attributes; these are His nature. This is how He happens to be, and He cannot be otherwise. Whether you are close to Him, whether you are standing opposite Him or turning your back on Him, He is the same.

It is just as with light. Even if your eyes are closed and you have never known the light, the light is there. It will not go into nonexistence just because your eyes are closed. Open your eyes! The light is there; it has always been there. Begin with your eyes, not with the light.

You cannot think about the light. You have never known it, so how can you think about it? Any thinking, any contemplating will be wrong; from the very beginning it will be wrong. You cannot think about something you have not known. Thinking about what is known can go on and on in circles, but it can never touch the unknown, it can never conceive of the unknown. The unknown cannot be thought about.

Thinkers go on denying God because He is not known to them. When someone says, "God is not," it is not that he is against God. It is only that he is a man who thinks; it is nothing else. He is not against God, because to be against God will have to be preceded by knowing Him. He is not against God, one who knows God cannot be against Him. How can one who has known God be against God? He cannot be. To say that God is not only shows that the man has not known God; he has only been thinking about Him. And through thinking you cannot conceive of the unknown, so the thinker denies it.

Do not begin with God; that is a false beginning. It always leads to nonsense. All metaphysics is nonsense. It goes on thinking about things that cannot be thought about. It goes on giving statements about the existence when no statements can be given. Only silence can be a statement about it. But if you begin with yourself, then much that is solid can be said. If you begin with yourself, then something scientific can be done. If you begin with yourself, then you begin at the right beginning.

Religion means to begin with oneself and metaphysics means to begin with God. So metaphysics is madness—of course, madness with a method. All madmen are metaphysicians without a method and all metaphysicians are mad, but with a methodology. Because of their methodology they seem to be talking sense—and they go on talking nonsense!

Begin with yourself. Do not ask whether God exists; ask

whether *you* exist. Do not ask whether love is an attribute of the divine; ask whether love is an attribute of yours, whether you have ever loved. Do not ask about grace; ask whether you have ever felt gratitude. Because that is nearer to you, because it is just a step away from you, you can know it.

Always begin from the beginning. Never begin from the end, because then there is no beginning at all. One who begins from the beginning always reaches the end, and one who begins from the end does not even reach the beginning. To begin from the end is impossible: you just go on and on in circles.

Don't let God be a metaphysical notion but, rather, a religious experience. Go inward. He is always there waiting for you. But then you have to do something with yourself. That doing is meditation; that doing is yoga.

Do something with yourself. As you are, you are closed; as you are, you are dead. As you are, you cannot be in a dialogue with the divine, with existence. So transform yourself: open some doors, break open some space, make some windows. Jump outside your mind, your past. Then it is not only that you will know the divine; you will live it. You will live with the grace of the divine; you will live with the love of the divine. You will be a part of it, just a ripple in it. And once you have become a ripple in it, a wave of the divine, only then is there authentic divineness.

So I am not a metaphysician at all. You can call me an anti-metaphysician. Religion is existential. Begin from yourself; begin transforming your aggressive mind. Just be receptive, open.

I would like to tell you that Buddha tried continuously for six years to know what the divine is. It cannot be said that he left anything undone. He did everything that is humanly possible, even some things that seem humanly impossible. He did everything. Whatever was known in his day he practiced, and whatever methods were taught to him he became a master of.

He went to all the gurus that existed in his time, to everyone. Whatever they could teach him, he learned, he practiced. Then he would say, "Anything more, sir?"

The guru would say, "Now you can go. All that I could give you, I have given. And I cannot say, as I might be able to say in other cases, that you have not practiced. You have practiced well. This is all that I can give."

Then Buddha would say, "But I have not known the divine yet."

With each guru this happened. Finally, he left all gurus. He invented his own methods. Continuously for six years he was in a life-and-death struggle. He did everything that could be done. At last he was so tired of doing, so deadly tired, that one day when he was taking his evening bath in the Niranjana River near Bodh Gaya he felt so weak and so tired that he could not come out of the river. He just clung to the root of a tree. A thought came to his mind: "I have become so weak that I cannot even cross this small river. How will I be able to cross the whole ocean of existence now? I have done everything and I have not found the divine—I have only tired my body."

He felt that he was on the verge of death. He felt that he had done everything and now there was nothing left to do. He relaxed, and the very moment he relaxed a new energy came into him. All that had been suppressed throughout those six years flowered. He came out of the river. He felt as light as a feather, a bird's feather —weightless. He relaxed under the bodhi tree.

It was a bright full-moon night. Someone came—a girl, a *shudra* girl named Sujata. Her name shows that she must have been a *shudra*. Sujata means "well-born," and only someone from a lower caste would be given a name meaning "well-born."

Sujata had promised to pay homage to the bodhi tree daily, so she had come with some sweets. Buddha was there, tired, pale, lifeless, but relaxed, absolutely unburdened. It was a full-moon night with nobody around. Sujata, seeing Buddha, felt that he was the deity of the tree, come to receive her homage. Had it been another day, Buddha would have refused. He would never rest at night; he would never eat anything. But on this night he was totally relaxed. He took the food and he slept. It was the first night in six years that he really slept.

He was relaxed, with nothing to do. Now there were no worries. There was no tomorrow for him—because tomorrow exists only when one has to do something. If one does not have anything to do, then there is no tomorrow. Then the present moment is enough.

Buddha slept, and at five o'clock in the morning when the last star was withering away, he awoke from his sleep. With an empty mind, with no-mind, he saw the last star disappearing from the sky. When you have nothing to do, there is no mind; the mind is just a faculty for doing something, it is a technical faculty. With no mind—with nothing to do, with no effort on his part, indifferent to whether he was alive or dead—he opened his eyes. And he began to dance! He had come to that knowing to which he could not come through much effort.

Whenever someone asked him how he had achieved, he would always say, "The more I tried to achieve, the more I was at a loss. I could not achieve. So how can I say I have achieved? The more I tried, the more 'I' was involved—I could not achieve." The mind was trying to transcend itself, which is impossible. It is just like trying to be a father to yourself, just like trying to give birth to yourself.

So Buddha would say, "I cannot say I achieved. I can only say I tried so much that I was annihilated. I tried so much that any effort became absurd. And a moment came when I was not trying —when the mind was not, when I was not thinking. Then there was no future because there was no past." Both are always together: past is behind, future is in front. They are always joined to one another: if one drops, the other drops simultaneously. "Then there was no future, no past—no mind. I was mindless, I was I-less. Then something happened. I can only say that it is always happening, but I was not aware of it before. I cannot say that it happened in that moment. It was always happening, only I was closed.

"So I cannot say I have achieved something," Buddha would say. "I can only say I have lost something: the ego, the mind. I have not achieved anything at all. Now I know that all that I have achieved was always there. It was everywhere—it was in every stone, in every flower. Now I recognize that it has always been so. Before, I was blind. I have simply lost my blindness. I have not achieved anything; I have lost something."

If you begin with the divine, then you begin with an achieving attitude. If you begin with yourself, then you begin with a losing attitude. Things will begin to disappear and ultimately *you* will disappear. And when you are not, the divine *is*—with all its grace, with all its love, with all its compassion.

But only when you are not. Your nonexistence is the categorical condition. For no one can this condition be relaxed. It is categorical; it is absolute. *You* are the barrier. When you disappear, you will know—and only when you know, you *know*. You cannot understand it. I cannot explain it to you, I cannot make you understand it.

No matter what I am saying, I am not saying anything metaphysical. I am only trying to show you that you must begin with yourself. And if you begin with yourself, you will end with the divine, because that is your other part, the other pole. But begin from this bank; do not begin from the other, where you are not. You cannot begin from there. Begin from where you are.

The deeper you go, the less you will be. The more you know yourself, the less you will be a self, and once you have come to a total understanding about yourself, you will be annihilated. You will go into nonexistence, you will be a total negativity. You will be *not*. And in that *not*, in that total negation, you will know the grace that is always falling, that is always raining down from eternity. You will know the love that is always around you. It has always been there, but you have not paid any attention to it. Be annihilated, and you will become aware of it.

5

Meditation: A Subtle Death

Bhagwan, how does meditation really work and in what way does kundalini *practice relate to meditation? How can one achieve a constant meditative state?*

Meditation is an adventure, an adventure into the unknown—the greatest adventure that the human mind can take. And by adventure I mean that you cannot be cultivated in it. First, you cannot know anything about it beforehand. Unless you *know* it, you cannot know it. Everything that can be said ultimately means nothing: the truth remains unsaid. Much has been said—much has been said about nothing. However, not a single word has been uttered.

Unless you *know* it, you cannot know it. But something about it can be indicated. It will never be to the point; it cannot be. The nature of the thing is such that this is impossible. You cannot say that *this* is meditation. All that is possible to say is that this is not meditation, that is not meditation. The remaining is—and the remaining is left unindicated.

There are many reasons for it. Meditation is something greater than the mind. It is not something that happens in the mind; it is something that happens *to* the mind. Otherwise the mind would be capable of defining it, of knowing it, of understanding it. So it is not something happening in the mind but to the mind. The happening is just like death happening to life. Death never happens *in* life; it happens *to* life.

Meditation is a death to the mind, just as death is to the body, to life. Meditation is a deeper death—not physical, but psychic. And the deeper the death, the deeper the possibility is to be reborn.

When there is physical death, you will be reborn physically. As far as your innerness is concerned, nothing will have happened, nothing at all. You will remain the same—the same continuity will be there; nothing will be different. But the deeper the death, the deeper the resurrection. If you die psychologically, if the mind dies, then too you are reborn, but the rebirth is not like physical rebirth. When the body dies it is replaced; a new body replaces it. But when there is mental death, psychic death, the mind is not replaced. Now consciousness remains without the mind.

Meditation is consciousness without the mind—an open sky without any walls around it. We can destroy the walls of a house but not the room, because room means nothing but space. Without the walls, the room will be "roominess." It will still be there under the open sky. Of course, you will no longer see it as a room because now you cannot define it—it has become one with the sky—but the room is still there, as much as before. Rather, it is more than before. Only the walls are not there. If you define the room as the walls, you will say that now there is no room, but if you define the room as the roominess, the emptiness between the walls, then without the walls the room will still be there. In fact, it will have become greater—infinite.

When the mind dies—that is, when the walls of the mind disappear—the emptiness within the walls, this space, remains, becomes greater. That is consciousness. I make a distinction: I call the emptiness within "consciousness" and the walls around it "the mind." Or you can say it like this: mind with a small *m* dies; Mind with a capital *M* goes on living.

Then it is not *your* mind; it cannot be yours. If the walls around this room are removed, I cannot say that the room is mine. The room will be there but it will not be mine because I can call "mine" only that which is within walls, within limitations. Pure emptiness cannot be mine. So when the mind with a small *m* dies and the Mind with a capital *M* is there, you are *not* there. And you are not replaced by any other mind; you are not replaced at all.

Meditation is a subtle death, but a deep one. It is the death of *you:* of your mind, of your ego, of all that defines you. Only what is within, what is not the mind, not the ego, remains—and that is pure consciousness.

So first of all, the walls of the mind, the mental processes, are not meditation. They are the obstacles to meditation. What are these walls? How has the mind defined itself, how has it become limited? What are the boundaries because of which the mind has become separated from Mind, from consciousness?

There are three things. The first is memory. The greater part of the mind is memory. And this memory is a long one; it goes back to the infinite lives you have lived. The mind accumulates everything, not only what you have collected consciously. When the child is in the womb, the mind is collecting. When you are asleep, the mind is collecting; even when you are in a coma, completely unconscious, the mind is collecting. The mind goes on collecting; nothing escapes it. The unconscious mind is a Great China Wall of memories—a very long one.

This memory is not only a part of your brain but, in fact, a part of each and every cell of your being, of each and every cell of your body. In the beginning, twenty-four cells from the male and twenty-four cells from the female created you. They had a built-in program, a built-in memory. One day we will even be capable of knowing, from the first day you are in the womb, what type of nose you will have. The new egg will indicate what type of eyes you will have, how old you will live to be, how much intelligence you will have, how much ego.

The simple-looking cell that you began life with is as complex as you are. It contains all the memories of the whole race; it carries within it the whole collective mind. Then your soul—your ego, your mind—penetrates in it. So the body has its own memories and your mind has its own memories. You are the crossroads: a mind with so many memories and a body with the memories of the whole collective race, the whole collective mind.

Bodily memories are stronger than the mind, so you are always a victim to them. However you may try to be against them, when the moment comes, the body wins. Your mind is nothing before it because the body is part of the racial mind. That is why all religions fell into a trap when they began to fight the body. You cannot fight it. If you begin to fight it, you will only be wasting your life.

You cannot fight with the body because your body is the whole race—and not only the race, it is the whole history of existence itself. Everything goes on living in you. Everything that has existed goes on living in your body; your self carries everything within it. That is why a child in the womb has to pass through all the stages the human being passes in evolution. Those nine months in the womb are the total evolution compressed. One begins just as an amoeba, the first primitive cell. One begins in the same situation that the amoeba had to begin in—in sea water. The womb contains the same chemical conditions as sea water, the same. The water in the womb in which the cell swims has the same components as sea water, exactly the same.

Evolution begins again in the womb, but of course it is a miniature evolution. The whole thing has to begin again because the cell has a memory. Unless it again goes through the whole evolutionary process, it cannot function as an evolved human cell. The time the process takes will be short: the amoeba had to wait millions of years before it was able to leave the sea, but this cell, this egg cell within the womb, will pass through this phase within a week. Within those seven days the same evolution will be there, the same evolutionary stages—millions of years compressed. The nine months in the womb are compressed evolution, and through that process the cell has a built-in program.

So in a way your body is the whole evolution. In a very compressed, atomic state, the body has a memory of its own, and one who wants to move into meditation will first have to understand his body memory, the physiological memory.

Do not fight with the body. If you begin fighting you are taking the wrong step and you will only be more and more disturbed. Be cooperative; there is no other way. Let the body be completely at ease; do not create any tension between you and the body. Your real fight is not with the body, not with the body memory, but with ego memory—your psyche, your mind—and that is another thing, completely different.

So do not fight with the body. When you fight with the body, you never have time to fight with the mind. When you begin to fight with the body it will go on and on; it will be suicidal. It will be destructive. It will just sow seeds of its own defeat. One is bound to be defeated. A single cell fighting the whole humanity, fighting the whole being as such! It is impossible.

So do not take bodily memories as your memories. For example, hunger is a body memory. You can fight with it, but to win will be very difficult, very arduous, nearly impossible. And if you win, your victory will be your total defeat. If you can win over your hunger you have taken a suicidal step: within ninety days you will be dead. Even the body will not indicate to you that now is the time to feed it. So it is better if you never win over your body. Otherwise it will be suicidal: there will be no bridge between you and your body memories. That is the only way to win. But you are not winning really. You are going to murder yourself.

There are methods that can break the bridge between you and your body. There are methods, so many hatha yoga methods, to break the bridge. The body goes on crying, "Hunger! hunger! hunger!" but you never know; the bridge is broken. The body goes on calling for attention but you never know about it. You have become insensitive to it.

Never practice anything that makes your body, or you, insensitive. Meditation is a total sensitivity. When you become meditative, your body will become so sensitive that right now you cannot even conceive of how sensitive it can be. We never hear exactly, we never see exactly—just so-so. You pass through a garden. You seem to be looking, but you just look, you do not see. The eyes have become insensitive: you have been fighting with the eyes. The body has become insensitive: you have been fighting with the body.

The whole culture is against the body, this whole culture— wherever it is, East or West, makes no difference. The culture that has developed on this planet is, in a way, diseased. It is against the body. But if you go against the body, then in a way you have gone against the universe. It is a miniature universe. Your relationship to the universe, your bridge to the universe, your instrument to reach out to the universe is through the body. The body is a great mystery.

So do not fight with the body. Always make a clear distinction between what is body memory and what is mind memory. Hunger is a body memory, but the mind also has its own memories. They are not existential; they have no survival value. That is the basic distinction between body memories and mind memories. Body memories have a survival value. If you deny them, if you fight against them, you will not survive. But psychological memories have no survival value really. They are simply an accumulation, a waste product—something that has to be thrown if you have accumulated it, something that needs to be thrown because you have burdened yourself with it. But these mind memories, too, are old, ancient.

Whenever you are angry there are two possibilities: it may be a body memory or it may be a mind memory. A certain distinction must be made between body memory and mind memory. If your anger has a survival value, if you cannot survive without it, then it is a bodily function. But if your anger has no survival value then it is just a habit of the mind, just a mechanical repetition of the mind. Then it is a mind memory. You have been angry so many times that it has become a conditioning with you. Whenever someone pushes the button, you are again angry. Just be aware of it.

And one who is never mentally angry, not habitually angry—

his bodily anger will have a beauty of its own. It will never be ugly. Then it will only be an indication that the person is living, not dead. The more you are habitually angry, the less will be your capacity to be bodily angry. Then your anger will just be ugly. It will not add anything to you. It will just be disturbing to yourself and to others.

We can understand it from another route also, for example, sex. Sex can be a bodily memory. Then it has a survival value. But it can also be just mental, cerebral, just out of habit. Then it has no survival value. If sex is just a habit it will become an ugly thing. It will have neither love nor beauty in it. Nor will it have any music or any deeper resonances. The more cerebral the sex, the less capable your body will be in it. You will think about it more, but you will not be able to know what it is exactly, what is its deepest mystery. The mind will go on thinking about sex and the body will have to follow.

Whenever the body follows the mind, there is no life in it. The body is just dragged along like a dead weight. With anything— sex, anger, greed, anything—always make a distinction as to whether or not it has survival value. If it has survival value, you do not have to fight with it.

If it is just a mental habit, then be aware of it. The memory of the mind, the memory of all your past actions, has become a conditioned thing. You go on repeating the past; you act just like a machine. Be conscious of this!

You will be surprised to know that if there is no mind in your anger—if it is just a total response to a situation, a response of the whole body, with no mental preconditioning—then there will be no repentance. You have acted totally in the situation, as the situation required. Then there need be no repentance at all. And when there is no repentance, there will be no psychological accumulation. Nothing will become a habit with you.

You need not accumulate anything. Why does the mind need to accumulate memories? Because it is not confident as to whether it can act totally in a situation. It prepares, it goes through many rehearsals. If there is such-and-such a situation, it is not confident of what it will do. It must know everything that has been done in similar situations. It must sort things out; it must develop a program of what is to be done in a particular situation. That is why the mind accumulates memories. But the more it accumulates, the less is its capacity to act totally. And the less its capacity to act totally, the more the mind will be needed.

So act with the body, do not act with the mind. It will look strange that I have said this—like something never expected from a religious man. Still I say it: act from the body! Then the response is total; the act is total. Do not let the mind come in and there will be no memory. There will be no mental accumulation; there will be no repentance. The act will be finished. Things were such —the situation was such—and you acted totally, with no part remaining behind. Now there is nothing to repent of and there is no one who can repent. You were totally in the act. It is the part that is held back that repents later on.

Body can act totally; mind can never act totally. Mind is always divided; mind works in dichotomies. One part of the mind is angry; another part is simultaneously repenting or preparing to repent. This should be noted: whenever one part of you is fighting against another part, you are acting through the mind and not through the body. Body is always total. It cannot act dividedly.

Body is just a flow; there are no divisions. When you fall in love, it is the whole body that has fallen in love. You cannot make a distinction that the head has fallen in love or that the hands have begun to love. The whole body is in it. But the mind can never be totally in anything. A part of it will always be criticizing, judging, condemning, appreciating; a part of it will always be sitting outside to judge, to condemn. So whenever you see that part of your mind is working against what you are doing, know that you are doing it cerebrally, mentally.

Begin to do things bodily. When you are eating, eat bodily. The body knows well when to stop, but the mind never knows it. One part will go on eating and another part will go on condemning. One part will go on saying, "Stop!" and another part will go on eating. The body is total, so ask the body. Do not ask the mind whether to eat or not to eat, to stop or not to stop. Your body knows what is needed. It has accumulated the wisdom of centuries and centuries. It knows when to stop.

Do not ask the mind; ask the body. Rely on the body's wisdom. The body is wiser than you. This is why animals live more wisely than we do. They live more wisely but, of course, they do not think. The moment they think, they will be just like us. They do not think, but just go on living wisely. And this is a miracle: that animals can live more wisely than human beings. It seems absurd. They know nothing, but they go on living more wisely.

The only ability in which the human being has become efficient is to interfere with everything. You go on interfering with your body. Do not interfere. Let the body work; do not get in its way. Then you will have a clear distinction of what is mental memory and what is body memory.

Body memory is a help toward survival; mental memory is obstructive. This mental memory must be destroyed. When I say destroyed, I do not mean that you will not remember anything. When I say to destroy the memory, I mean that you should not be identified with the memory, you should not become one with it. The memory must not be an autonomous affair; it must not perpetuate itself.

It goes on perpetuating itself. You are just sitting and your memory is working; you are sleeping and the memory is working; you are working at your job and the memory is working. The memory goes on continuously working. What is it doing?

What can memory do? Memory can only desire what it knows for the future. It can do nothing else. It can perpetuate and project itself into the future. All that has been should be again; or something that has been should not be. Memory is always weaving a pattern for the future around you, and once you allow it to weave a pattern for you, you will never be free. You will always be functioning according to pattern.

That pattern is the wall that surrounds the emptiness of consciousness. Before you take one step into the future, your memory has taken many steps. Now the path is not an open path; it has become an imprisonment. Memory is always narrowing your path, but you are deceived by it because you think that it is helping you to live a better future. It is not helping. It is just helping you to make your future the same as the past.

The memory cannot project anything that it has not known. It can only project the known: it *will* project it. Do not fall into the trap. Do not allow the mind to project for the future even for a moment. Of course, it will take time for you to learn to be without this dead habit, but to begin to be aware of it is meditation. And once you are aware—completely aware, intensely aware, alert—the memory will not weave the future for you.

Memory can weave the future for you only when you are dreaming. To be dreaming is a basic condition for the memory to work. That is why in sleep the dreams that are created are so real, more real than reality. When you are just sitting in your easy chair, daydreams begin, reveries begin. Anytime you are just a little sleepy your memory begins to work, it begins to project. Be alert, conscious, and the memory stops projecting into the future.

Alertness—more alertness within and without—is the beginning of meditation. This alertness can be created in many ways. By telling you to be alert I know that you are not going to become alert. You will hear this in a dreaming state and the memory will project it: "Yes, I will be alert tomorrow." The memory will pick up what I have said and project it. If you hear me say to be alert, you will make it a projection. You will say, "Yes, I will be alert sometime." If I say that happiness comes to you through alertness, if I say that bliss is bound to come to you through alertness, you will be even more dreamy—the memory will project what I have said into the future.

My telling you to be alert will not make you meditative. It will not make any difference. So I create devices; I create situations in which you cannot help but be alert—situations in which dreaminess is impossible.

I will tell you something. Dreaminess becomes more possible

if there is more carbon dioxide around you. You will be more dreamy. That is why in the day you will not be so dreamy as in the night. The chemical components change. There is more carbon dioxide in the air and less oxygen. If the reverse is possible —if a situation can be created where there is more oxygen in you and around you and less CO_2—then you will not be so dreamy. That is why in my technique of Dynamic Meditation I insist on vigorous breathing.* It is nothing but a chemical device: to change the chemical atmosphere in you. The more oxygen there is in you, the less you can fall victim to dreaming. And your memory cannot project without a certain amount of dreaminess.

In the morning we feel fresh. What happens in the morning as the sun rises? The amount of CO_2 in the air decreases and the oxygen increases. To make you more alert, more aware, this same chemical change has to take place within you. The technique that I am teaching now at the meditation camps—Dynamic Meditation—is the most powerful method there is to create excess oxygen in the body. After the first three vigorous stages of the technique, in the fourth stage one becomes charged with tremendous life energy, which makes one very alert.

Another device to make you alert is *kundalini* practice. It is a system of transforming sex energy into meditation and awareness. But it is most useful to a person whose sex energy can be easily and naturally channeled into meditation. In the days of the Vedas and Upanishads in ancient India, the people were simple and natural and they could easily convert their sex energy into meditation. For them, sex was not a mental problem; it was not a problem at all. Once it becomes mental, it becomes a problem.

*Dynamic Meditation, a technique devised by Bhagwan Shree and practiced daily at Rajneesh Meditation Centers around the world, begins with ten minutes of deep, fast breathing through the nose. There is no rhythm to the breathing. The emphasis is that it be as deep and as fast as possible. Ten minutes of catharsis, of spontaneously expressing whatever energy breathing has created, follows. The third ten-minute step is the vigorous repetition of the sufi mantra *hoo*. One is to exhaust oneself completely so that one can be totally passive, totally vulnerable in the fourth stage, the meditation. For a complete description of Dynamic Meditation and other techniques devised by Bhagwan Shree, see *Meditation: The Art of Ecstasy* (New York: Harper & Row, 1976).

The modern world is so sexually perverse and sexually exploited that to work with *kundalini* energy has become difficult. But through Dynamic Meditation *kundalini* is sometimes felt to be rising. If someone feels his *kundalini* rising, then I begin to work on his *kundalini*. Then I begin to give him techniques for working on it. But unless there is a spontaneous feeling of *kundalini*, I will not even talk about it. You can bypass *kundalini*, and it may be that today you will have to bypass it. Only with natural sex, with physical sex—with sex that is not a function of the mind—can *kundalini* work. Only with innocent minds can it work.

But somewhere on the way, when you have gone deeper into meditation, your mind loses its grip. As I have said to you, when you go deeper into meditation, you learn to make a distinction between body memory and mind memory. When there is a distinction and a separation between these two memories, then you become less and less mental about the body and you can let the body function by itself, through its own wisdom. Then sometimes, by itself, *kundalini* will become active.

If *kundalini* begins to work automatically, it is good; but I don't suggest that you work with *kundalini* directly. Indirectly, it will begin to work by itself. It happens so many times: at least thirty to forty percent of the people who are practicing Dynamic Meditation feel *kundalini*. When they feel it, I am ready; then they can proceed. Then, by this method, they can proceed through the door of *kundalini*.

But this method, Dynamic Meditation, is only indirectly connected to *kundalini*. And as far as I am concerned, it will not be possible to use direct *kundalini* methods in the future unless the whole world begins to take sex as a natural phenomenon. Then, too, there are no *kundalini* techniques that are used before sexual maturity. But unless the path for *kundalini* to move is created within you before sexual maturity, there is every possibility that, even if sex is taken naturally and you do not turn out to be a pervert, you may turn out to be no different from an animal.

I will tell you a story from the Upanishads. A *rishi* is sitting with his wife and son. A man passes by. He falls in love with the wife and asks her to accompany him to his residence. The wife goes away with the man. There is no criticism or objection from the *rishi.*

The son becomes angry. He says to his father, "This is just animalistic. This is just what animals do; this cannot be allowed. I have a moral code; I cannot allow this. This is just what animals do!"

The father says, "This is not just like animals. On the contrary, your rage, your anger, is just what animals do. It is a projection of moral violence: it is just like an animal. No animal will allow what has happened to happen. If he can fight, he will fight. But no animal can hold onto a possession forever."

This attitude, the father's attitude, is really a higher one. It cannot be understood. He says, "Your attitude is just like an animal's." Animals fight for their mates; they have a territorial, possessive sense. They will not allow you in their territory, whether it is for sex or for food or for anything. They have a territorial sense. If you trespass it, they will fight.

But the father says, "This is human. If somebody sees your mother and falls in love, no one is at fault. And if your mother is ready, who am I? I have also fallen in love with her just like this. It is no different. I fell in love with her in the same way. She agreed to be married to me, she agreed to be my wife—but not my possession. Now someone else has fallen in love with her. I know human weakness because I know myself. I have fallen in love with her myself. Nothing wrong is happening. And I am not an animal so I cannot fight about it. I know the man is a human being just like me. And your mother is beautiful. I have also fallen in love with her."

But this is a very high morality. It can be cultivated only if you have been trained before sexual maturity, otherwise not. After sexual maturity you will not be able to learn to channel the energy. It is very difficult to rechannel the energy, but if the channels are ready beforehand then the energy flows in them as naturally as it flows in sex. This man—this father, this *rishi*—must have known *kundalini* or he could not be as he was; it is impossible.

This *rishi* had developed his *kundalini;* his energy was moving upward. Otherwise, this attitude would never have come. Downward energy is always toward violence; upward energy is always toward love, understanding, compassion.

So this method of Dynamic Meditation is an indirect method. It works through many doors. If your *kundalini* can be used, the method will use it; it will take the route of *kundalini.* The method is flexible, absolutely flexible. If your *kundalini* is not ready to be used, if it is dangerous to use it, then it will not be used in the technique. Then there are other channels, other routes; the method can work through other routes.

There are no names for these other routes because no ancient teaching used them. But there are other routes. Mahavir never talked about *kundalini.* Buddha never talked about *kundalini.* Christ never knew about it, Lao Tzu never heard about it. They proceeded through other routes.

The way for Buddha could not have been through *kundalini.* Sex had become absolute boredom to him; he was not in the least interested in sex. And that was bound to happen because his father had arranged for so many beautiful girls to be around him. Every girl who was beautiful was there in his palace. Finally, he just became disgusted with sex.

It was bound to happen. Everyone will become disgusted like that, everyone in Buddha's place will become disgusted. He became so disgusted with sex that he could not conceive that this same energy could be converted. He never tried it. Even if someone had said to him that sex energy can become divine energy, he would not have listened. He had known sex so much and to him there had been nothing divine about it; it had just been carnal. So Buddha used another route; he did not talk about *kundalini* at all. But he talked about centers, *chakras.* He worked with *chakras.*

If you work with *kundalini* it is a gradual process. *Kundalini* is a continuity. It has a continuity just like a thermometer; it rises like a thermometer. It rises—slowly, slowly. The passage is a continuous one. Buddha never used that passage, but he talked about *chakras—chakras* working in sudden jumps. From one *chakra* you jump to another; there is no continuity. One just jumps.

Because of this jumping process, Buddha conceived of the whole world in a very new way. He said there is no continuity in the world, only jumps. Nothing is continuous. The flower is not continuous with the bud; the flower is a jump. Youth is not a continuity of childhood; it is a jump.

Buddhist philosophers are very happy now because today science also says that there is no continuity, Everything jumps; there is a jump. We see continuity only because we cannot see the gaps between.

You see this light continuously. It is not continuous. Electrons are jumping, but the gaps are so small that your eyes cannot know them. It is not continuous, it is jumping; but the jumps are so quickly taken that when one electrical particle is dead and the other has come, the gap between is not noticed. There is a sudden jump. You light a flame in the evening and in the morning when you put it out, you think that you are putting out the same flame. The flame has jumped thousands of times. It has gone, evaporated, and a new flame has come. But it looks continuous.

Heraclitus said that you can never step in the same river twice. Because the river is flowing, you can never step in it twice. Buddha will say that you cannot even step in it once because it is flowing and as soon as you have touched the surface it is gone. Before you have gone deeper into it, it is gone. Even one step and so many rivers have gone!

This jumping concept came to Buddha because he never passed through *kundalini.* His movement was a jump from one *chakra* to another, so he talks about seven *chakras.* That, too, is possible. I can walk to your house or I can come to your house by jumping. Then I touch only certain points. There are gaps; there is no continuity.

Mahavir never talks about either *chakras* or jumps. He talks about explosions. You are "this" and then suddenly you are "that" —there is an explosion. It is not even that there are many stations to jump to. There is another route altogether, an explosion. You explode; you just explode. One moment you are "this" and the next moment you are "that." There is neither a continuity nor a jump; there is an explosion. There is no midpoint to be crossed.

There are two sects of Zen. One sect is known as the sudden school of Zen and the other is the gradual school of Zen. But even gradual Zen does not talk about *kundalini.* It has used another route, so there is no talk about *kundalini* in Zen. Another route has been used.

The body has many routes. It is a great world in itself. You can work through breathing, and through breathing you can take the jump. You can work through sex, and through sex you can take the jump. You can work through awareness—that is, directly through consciousness—and you can take the jump. This working directly on consciousness has been one of the deepest routes.

But even one single route can be used in many ways. You must understand the complexity of this. For example, one road can be used in many ways: one can use it with a car, another with a bullock cart, another just by walking. The route is the same, but the method is absolutely different. What is common between walking and sitting in a car? Nothing is common. In the car you are just sitting and not doing anything. If someone says, "I passed over this road just by sitting," he is not saying anything false, but one who has only walked, and who has never known how it is possible to move along the road just by sitting, will deny that this can be done. Yet this method, too, is right.

So even a single route can be used in different ways, for example, awareness. Gurdjieff used it, but he called it self-remembering. The route is the same, but the method is different. Consciousness is to be used directly, but as self-remembering, not as awareness.

What is the difference between the two? Self-remembering means that when you are walking on the street, just remember you are. Stand for a moment: remember you are. Look around, completely remembering you are. Never forget for a single moment that you *are.*

We go on forgetting; we never remember. If I see you, I forget myself and see you. The awareness becomes one-arrowed; the other arrow is not there. Gurdjieff says to make awareness double-arrowed. You are listening to a discourse. To listen to what the speaker says is the first arrow. If you are also aware of yourself— that is, aware of the listener—then that is the second arrow. Do not forget yourself when you are listening; remember that you are listening. Someone is speaking and you are listening. Be beyond both—and remember. Make yourself double-arrowed. The route is the same, but the method is different.

But Krishnamurti will say, "Do not remember this way. It will become a tense effort. Just be aware of the totality. Do not choose by thinking that you are here and the other is there. Do not choose; just let there be an all-inclusive awareness. Do not focus on it: an unfocused awareness." I am speaking, you are sitting, the car horn outside is blowing, the car is passing—things *are,* and awareness is unfocused. Do not make the focus arrowed; make it unfocused. The route is the same, but the method is quite different.

Tantra used the same method, the same route, but in a different way. It was unimaginable. They used intoxicants: *bhang, charas, ganja,* wine. And the method was this: to take the intoxicant and be aware. Do not lose awareness. Go on taking the intoxicant and be aware that you are aware. Do not lose consciousness. And there are methods in which no intoxicant will have any effect. Even snake poison was used. A snake is made to bite you on the tongue. If the snake bites you on the tongue and you remain aware, only then have you taken the jump, otherwise not. The route is the same, but the method is quite different.

In this kind of tantric practice—if no intoxicants work and you go on remaining conscious, you behave consciously—then something has crystallized within you. Something has gone beyond body chemistry; otherwise the chemistry will affect you. Now you are beyond body chemistry. The chemistry is working somewhere in the body, but you are aloof. It cannot touch you.

There are many routes, and each route can be used with many

methods. Dynamic Meditation is not directly concerned with any route. It is like a vehicle that can fly or swim or move on the road. Whatever the need of your personality is, the need will change the method, the route. So you can call Dynamic Meditation a multimethod. It is indirect; it cannot be direct. I give you the method. Your body, your being, will provide the route.

The energy awakened through the method can use any route: tantric, Buddhist, Jain, Sufi, Gurdjieff's route. And when I say this, it is not just a hypothesis. When I say this it is because I have found that it works in this way. People have come to me who have worked on different routes. When they use this method it begins to help them on their particular path.

If someone is working on *kundalini* and he comes to me and begins to work with this method, it helps him on his own route. He says, "This method is wonderful. The previous *kundalini* method I was using is not working so intensely." And this is not a *kundalini* method at all! But the method is flexible; it will find the route that is right for you. You have only to *do* it and everything else will be done by the method itself.

For the coming world, and also for today's world, only such flexible methods can be used, because there are so many types of people now. In the old world that was not the case. In a particular region, a particular type existed. If there were Hindus, there were only Hindus; there were no Moslems. In fact, they never heard about one another. They never knew about each other's practices so they were never confused. They were of a single type. If they were Tibetan Buddhists, they were Tibetan Buddhists. They never heard about anything else. Everyone's conditioning was the same; everyone was brought up in the same milieu, so only one method that worked was needed.

Now it is very difficult. Minds are confused. Not only is there more than one type, but each individual himself is a multitype. There are many influences, contradictory influences. That is why all religions say, "Do not study other religions; do not go to other teachers." It is not simply dogmatism. It looks dogmatic, but basically the reason for it is just to prevent unnecessary confusion. If too many methods are tried, no method will be used fully.

But now everyone is confused, and there is nothing that can be done to prevent it. There is no single type to be protected from confusion. So now we need new methods that belong to no type and can be used by every type.

This method of Dynamic Meditation is flexible. I am not particularly concerned with *kundalini,* not particularly concerned with anything, but deeply concerned with everything. Use this method, and the method will find the route that can be used by you. I leave this to the method itself. The method discovers it, and discovers it more exactly than you can discover it for yourself.

This discovery happens unconsciously. The method just puts you in a situation that is like being in a house when the house catches on fire. You are in a crisis situation. If you can run, you run. If you can jump, you jump. The situation is there, and the situation will push you toward whatever is possible for you.

The unconscious mind always chooses the route of least resistence. That is the mathematics, the inner economy of the mind. You never unconsciously choose any long route; you always choose the shortest. Only with the conscious mind do you begin to choose routes that lead nowhere or are so long that you are dead before you reach them. But the unconscious always chooses the short route—the shortest. So this method will create the situation, and your unconscious will take the route that is potentially its type.

6
Spiritual Explosion: The Creation of the New

Bhagwan, you have said that whenever the ultimate spiritual explosion happens to a person there starts around him a process of spiritual explosion that affects other seekers, like a chain reaction. Has a chain reaction of spiritual explosion started around you? Are there people who are near you physically who are going to explode in the very near future?

First, one has to understand what is meant by spiritual explosion. Many things are implied in it. One, the explosion is something about which you cannot do anything directly. Your efforts are meaningless. It is not something that you can manage to cause; explosion just happens to you. You cannot do anything positively to create the explosion because if it is created by you it will not be an explosion at all. Then you will remain, you will continue. Even after the explosion, you will be there. If *you* have experienced the explosion, then the "you" has not exploded in it. So positively, no effort can be made toward explosion. This is the first thing, the first basic implication of explosion.

Explosion means a discontinuity with the past. The old has

gone completely and the new has come. There is no continuity between the two. This new is not connected with the old; there is no causal link, it is not caused by the old. If it is caused by the old, then there is no explosion. Then there is a continuity: the old has continued in a new form. Then you may have gained something, you may have added something to you, but you are the same; the central being remains the same. Only on the periphery has something been added and accumulated. Your ego becomes more strengthened, stronger than before—you become richer.

So in continuity, there is no explosion possible. Explosion means that the old has died completely, the new has come into being, and there is no causal link between the two. Only if there is a gap—an unbridgeable gap, an abyss—can you call it an explosion.

This is very difficult to understand. Everything in our lives is easy to understand because everything is causal. Our whole logical thinking is based on causality: everything is connected; everything is related and is in continuity with something else. Nothing is new. Everything is just a modification of the old, so it can be understood.

The mind is the continuity. The mind is filled with accumulated knowledge, with memory. It can always understand the old, but the new is incomprehensible to it. The new cannot be understood by the mind, and if your mind tries to understand the new, it will transform it into terms of the past. It will give shape to it, meaning to it, and will categorize it. Only if things are connected to the old can the mind be at ease, because only then can it understand.

Explosion is something that cannot be understood by the mind. In fact, in explosion the mind explodes and is thrown out completely. So the second thing to be understood is this: you will not be able to understand explosion. All that you can understand will not be explosion. You will try to change the phenomenon into something that is known, into something old.

You may think that what I mean by "explosion" is like any

other explosion, but spiritual explosion is not similar to any other phenomenon. If a bomb explodes, everything is destroyed; the old order is gone and there is chaos. But this chaos is caused by the old; it is a continuity. Nothing new has come into being. This whole chaos, this whole disorder, is just a continuity of the old order. Nothing new has come into being. It is just the old, in a disordered way.

So no material explosion can even be symbolic, or used metaphorically, for spiritual explosion. The word comes from a material happening and has a connotation that is quite misleading. Spiritual explosion does not mean that the old is disordered, that the old has become chaotic. Spiritual explosion means that something new is created, something new has come into being.

Material explosion is destructive; spiritual explosion is creative. If you try to understand what I mean by spiritual explosion through analogy, you will not be able to know it. Something new, something quite new, comes into being. You cannot give it meaning because you are the old. You cannot create it; you just have to be vacant. You can only help it negatively by your absence, by not being. If you are absent, then the explosion will take place. Your cooperation is needed only in a negative way.

To do something positively is easy, but to do something negatively is very arduous. To cooperate is easy, not to cooperate is easy, but to cooperate negatively is very difficult. To cooperate negatively means not to create hindrances—and we all go on creating hindrances to prevent the new from coming into being.

We always emphasize the old, we always stick to the old, are identified with the old. The old is the "I." When I say the "I," I mean it is the total past. So how can I help the new? How can I help the future if "I" am the past? Whenever I say "I," it is the whole past incorporated into a single word. All that is dead now, all that must be buried now, stands behind this "I." This "I" becomes a hindrance—the only obstacle, the only obstruction for the new to come in.

You cannot do anything with the "I" positively, but negatively you can do something. Understand that you are the old and let this understanding go deep, let it penetrate you to your innermost depths. Become completely aware that you cannot help the new to come into being. But unless the new comes in, there is no spirituality. Unless the new explodes, you will not be reborn, you will not be in the dimension of the divine.

It is not that I am to be freed. Rather, there will be freedom from the "I," freedom from myself. It is not that I am to do something; rather, I must not do anything so that this phenomenon can happen. We continue to do something or other. This insistence to do something comes out of the "me": it prolongs, it continues, the "me"; it projects "me" into the future. Then there can be no explosion.

The dead past, which accumulates like dust, goes on accumulating on your mirrorlike consciousness. Then the mirrorlike consciousness is lost and only the dust is seen; you become identified with the dust. Can you imagine yourself without your past? If your total past is destroyed, how will you live? What will you do? Who will you be? If everything from the past is taken away, by and by you will feel you are disintegrating and disappearing. When there is no past, who are you? Where are you? With what will you be identified then?

If there is no past you will still exist, but not in the same way. Really, you will be diametrically opposite to what you were. If the whole past is taken away, you will just be consciousness. Then you cannot be an ego. The ego is the accumulated events, the past. If it is taken away from you, you will have a new identity. You will be just like a mirror, mirroring everything.

Once you become aware that *you* are the hindrance, you do not have to do anything. This very awareness will destroy your old identity, and when the old identity is completely destroyed— when there is a gap between your real being and your memories, when there is a space between your ego and you—then, within that space, the explosion happens. Within that space is the explosion!

This explosion cannot be comprehended intellectually in any way whatsoever. The more you try to understand it, the less you will understand it. So do not be tense about it; just be relaxed. And do not try to understand me. Rather, feel what I am saying inside yourself. If I say you are the past, do not just hear my words and think about whether they are right or wrong. Go inside and *feel* what is being said.

Think in terms of facts. What I am saying is a fact. Go inside and see whether you are the past, see whether what I am saying is really a fact. Have you anything inside you that is other than the past? Are you just the dead past or is there something else living inside you that is not part and parcel of the past? What is it? You cannot confine it to yourself because the "I" is the confinement, the past is the confinement. You can confine the past because it is limited. The past can be confined: it has happened, it is finite. But if you become aware of something in you that is not of the past, but here and now, then even if the whole past is destroyed, it will still be. Even if you are not, it will still be.

If you find something in you that will not be destroyed by the destruction of the past but will continue to be, it is pure consciousness, a mirrorlike consciousness. You are not reflected in it; you are just a mirror that mirrors everything. Then you will feel the gap between your ego and you; you will feel the space.

If you can remain in this understanding, in this awareness, it becomes a meditation. If you can just remain in this understanding and awareness, in this space between your real being and your past, then the accumulated being, the ego, becomes just an outer layer. It becomes just a boundary line and in the center is pure consciousness.

Remain in this pure consciousness, in the center. It will not be easy, it will be very inconvenient and arduous, because we have never remained there. We always run to the periphery, we always become identified with the periphery. We live on the periphery and never in the center.

The periphery is the ego. All events happen on the periphery, on the circumference. The circumference is the point from which you are in touch with others.

If I love you, the happening of love is on the periphery because only my periphery can be in touch with and in contact with your periphery. Everything in this world happens on the periphery, on the boundary line, so we always remain on the boundary line. That is the field of activity.

But the being is always in the center. If you can remain in this gap, in this space—if you can exist in the center, not on the periphery, if you can become aware of the periphery as the dead part, as just the surface, just the body—the "you" is lost. I am not talking about the physical body. When I say "the body," I mean the ego.

If this space is not intellectually comprehended, not logically understood, but existentially felt, it will become inconvenient. You will become uneasy, as if you are dying. You have always remained on the periphery—that has been your life—so if you go back to your center it will be just like dying. At present the periphery has become your life; you do not know any other life. You will feel as though you are sinking, dying, as if you are suffocating. The mind will say, "Go back to the periphery. Life is there."

But on the periphery there is no life—only action. There is only doing, not being. That is why, when you do not have to do anything, not doing becomes so difficult that you cannot remain with it. You begin to do something. You may read a newspaper, you may put on the radio, you may do anything. Or if there is nothing to do, then you may go to sleep. But remaining in non-doing is the most arduous thing.

Not for a single moment do you remain in nondoing. But the being is revealed only to those who can remain in nondoing, who can remain in the center. That is what is meant by negative cooperation. Your cooperation is needed in a negative way: you are not to do anything; you are to remain in nondoing. Then the explosion takes place. It just happens to you.

You will always be in the center when it happens. This does not mean that now you will not be able to do anything. You will be able to do many things, but the quality of the action will be altogether different. A different kind of love will be possible from the center, a different kind of activity will be possible from the center. Now love will not be an act, but a state of mind. It will not be that sometimes you love and sometimes you do not love. Now it will become your very existence; you will be loving. Every action and every relationship will have a different quality, a different meaning, a different depth.

Through this explosion, you will become totally disidentified with the mind, with the ego, with the body, with the periphery —totally disidentified. Explosion is the destruction of the identification. Now nothing will be continuous with what went before, because all continuity is on the periphery. The explosion is not something continuous with the periphery. It is a jump.

If you go on running on the periphery it is a continuity. If you go round and round on the periphery you may run for a lifetime, but each step is bound with the previous one and each step leads you to the next. It is a linked process. But jumping from the periphery to the center is not continuous with the old. It is discontinuous. It is not caused by your previous steps; it is completely new and uncaused.

This becomes difficult to understand because in the world of happenings and events nothing is uncaused. But modern physics has come close to this point; it has come to a parallel situation. Because the behavior of the electron has been found to be discontinuous, physics has entered a new dimension. Prior to this century, physics was the system that was most based upon the scientific method. Everything was caused: everything was a continuity, everything was certain. Only with a causal link is there certainty; when things can happen uncaused, there is no certainty. Then there are really no laws that can be applied.

The whole science of physics is floundering today because they cannot determine the behavior of the electron. It behaves without causes. Sometimes it disappears from one point and then appears on another without any continuity between. From point A, the electron disappears. On point B, it appears—and there is no continuity between A and B. It has not been continuous; it has not traveled. This seems to be mysterious.

I use the behavior of the electron as an analogy. There are two types of thinking: one is logical thinking and the other is analogical thinking. Logical thinking proceeds in sequence: "this" is so; therefore "this" will happen. The cause is determined, so the effect will follow. The logical process is a definite, specific process: given a particular premise, a particular result will follow automatically. There is no freedom. Everything is caused by the past so it is dominated by the past. If I give you a particular amount of poison, you will die. You are not free: a particular amount of poison will cause death. Death *must* follow. It is a certainty, a continuity, a causal link.

Analogical thinking is quite different, altogether different. Analogical thinking is, in a way, poetic. You jump from one thing to another simply through analogy, not through logical sequences. For example, I may love someone and may write a poem in which I say, "My beloved is just like the moon." There is no connection: there is no causal link between the face of my beloved and the moon. There is no relationship at all, only analogy. I have jumped from one point to another without traveling between in any sequence. The behavior of the electron is just like this.

Poets have always been behaving like that. They jump from one point to another simply through analogy. There may not even be any obvious resemblance, but if it appears to the poet that somehow there is a resemblance, that is enough. There is a jump, an analogical jump.

The whole literature of mysticism is analogical. Mystics can only give you analogy. That is why there are so many parables. They are all analogical. Jesus was talking in analogies; so was Buddha and everyone else. They did not give any logical reasons or arguments. Jesus never argued about any point. There is no argument; it is just an analogy. Only if you are sympathetic can you understand analogical thinking. If you are not sympathetic then you cannot understand, because analogy depends not on reasoning but on your sympathetic attitude and on whether you can continue the same process inside yourself.

I use the behavior of the electron as an analogy for what happens when there is a spiritual explosion. The old remains on the periphery and there is no link between the periphery and the center. You cannot travel from the periphery to the center. If you could travel between the two, there would be a link from the periphery. Then the first step toward the center would be taken on the periphery and each step would be connected with the previous one. Then there would be a causal link between the center and the periphery. But if you are on the periphery and suddenly you find yourself at the center—and there is no travel between—that is an explosion.

Physics might not be known to you, so I will use another analogy. For example, you sleep in Bombay and dream that you are in London. In the morning when the dream is over, the sleep has gone, will you have to travel back to Bombay from London? While you were sleeping in Bombay, you dreamed that you were in London. If someone comes and wakes you up while you are dreaming you are in London, will you awaken in London or Bombay? Of course, you will awaken in Bombay. But how did you come back? Did you travel any distance? If you traveled from London to get back to Bombay, you would still be dreaming because the distance would have to be traveled only in a dream. If you travel the distance—if you take a plane—the plane will be part of the dream. But if you simply wake up, the dream will be discontinued in London. You will wake up in Bombay without having traveled there. The waking is something new; it is not continuous with the dream.

The periphery is the dream: the dream of doing, the dream of the ego. That is why mystics in India have said that the world is illusion. They have said, "It is just a dream; the whole world is just a dream." But when Shankara and others have said that this world is a dream, it is an analogy and must not be misunderstood. It has been misunderstood. You can point out what nonsense they are saying: "How can this world be a dream? It is so real!" The Indian mystic and philosopher Shankara also knew that the world is real, but he was talking in analogy.

"The world is a dream." When this is said, it does not mean that the world is actually a dream. It only means that if you are awakened, your previous awareness of the world, your previous perception of it, will be discontinued. You will not find any connection between dream and waking, you will not find any connection whatsoever, any relation whatsoever. You will just be bewildered as to how you were in London and how you came back.

But no one is bewildered really. When one is out of a dream, one is never bewildered. When you wake up, are you ever bewildered? You just say, "Oh, it was a dream," and the chapter is closed. You never think about it.

The same thing happens whenever there is an explosion. You know. You say, "The dreaming entity has dissolved. It was a dream and now I am at the center." You never ask how: how was I on the periphery and how did I come back to the center again? how did I travel? You never ask it.

People would ask Buddha, "How did you become enlightened?" The question is absurd. It is just like asking someone how he came out of a dream: what is the method? what is the technique? How can you practice coming out of a dream? The dream is just broken; a dream has its own way of being broken.

Sometimes a dream becomes a nightmare. It becomes unbearable. Then the very unbearableness of it, the anguish of it, causes it to break down. So if life on the periphery has become a nightmare, if living as you are living has become hellish, then all of this will awaken you from the dream. But when you are out of it, you will know that the awakening was not caused; there was no continuity. That is why we call it an explosion. Something new happens, something totally new. It cannot be understood in terms of the old.

What can you do to help the explosion to happen, even negatively? You can be aware—even if you can be aware only for a single moment. Be aware that you have become identified with a past that is not your being. The being is in the present, here and now, and you are identified with something that is not here and now. Be aware of this. Wherever you are, let this awareness suddenly come to you.

You are walking on the street. Stop for a moment and suddenly be aware. Anywhere, in any situation, stop for a moment and suddenly be aware of where you are—on the periphery or in the center? Are you identified with the memory or are you not identified with the memory? In the beginning this awareness will come only for a moment, or not even for a moment. There will just be a glimpse for a part of a moment. You will feel it, and it will be gone. But that glimpse will deepen and there will be a new movement from the periphery to the center, a movement just like the movement of an electron—a jump, a leap, from one point to another. The situation will deepen.

Remain aware as much as you can, and use every situation. For example, the breath has gone out and the breath has not yet come in. There is a gap—a very minute, very small gap between the two. Neither are you taking the breath in nor is the breath going out. Become aware of that gap! Remain in it for a single moment and you will feel the center. You will be far away from the periphery; you will be out of the dream.

You are going to sleep. Be aware that sleep is coming in. It is descending on you; you are sinking into it. Then there is a moment when you are neither awake nor asleep. The mind is changing its dimension: for a single moment you are neither asleep nor awake. Be aware of it, remain in that gap, and you will be thrown to the center; you will have jumped from the periphery. Then again in the morning when you are returning from a state of sleep, feel that moment when you have not yet become awake but sleep has gone. There is always one moment: whenever the mind changes from one state to another, there is a gap.

Everywhere, there is a gap. Without the gap, change is impossible. In that gap, you are never on the periphery; that gap is discontinuous with the periphery. You must understand exactly what I am saying. No gap is on the periphery; every gap is at the center.

All continuity is on the periphery. One event happens; then another event happens. And in between there is always a gap; you are always at the center. You always go back to the center and then the next moment you are back on the periphery, but this happening is so rapid, it is so timeless in a way, that ordinarily you cannot become aware of it. But if you become aware, attentive, watchful, careful, then by and by you will have glimpses.

You love someone. The love has gone and the hatred has not yet set in. There is a moment when neither exists. The love happens on the periphery, the hatred happens on the periphery, but the gap between them always happens at the center. So when you love you are on the periphery, when you hate you are on the periphery, but when you change from love to hate or from hate to love, you are not on the periphery. The gap is always at the center; you are thrown back to the center.

From the periphery you cannot change, because on the periphery there is only doing. The being is at the center. You must come back to the center in order to change, but this coming and going is so rapid, so timelessly rapid, that ordinarily you are not aware of it. So be alert in any change. You have been ill. Now the illness has gone but health is not yet there. Be aware! You will be at the center, because no change is possible on the periphery itself.

That is why everyone needs sleep. In sleep, a great change happens. If you cannot sleep deeply you will not be able to live, because life needs certain changes every day. Every day there is much that has to be changed in the body, in the mind, in the emotions. Much has to change every day, so nature has a way of making you unconscious—because consciously you cannot remain in the center for long. You are thrown into the unconscious so that you are not on the periphery. When you are asleep you are not running to the periphery. You are unconscious, so you are at the center, and you have settled in the being.

But even when you are awake, there are changes that you go through. An analogy is when you change the gears in your car. For a very short time you put the car in neutral. It is always through the neutral position that you change the gear. Neutral means "no gear." If you shift from first gear to second gear, you cannot shift it directly: the change needs to pass through a no-gear state. It must be put in neutral first, then it can be changed. The more expert you become, the less time it takes. Really, an expert driver becomes unaware that every time a gear is changed it passes through neutral. It is changed so swiftly that he need not be aware of it. Only one who is learning to drive is aware; no one is aware otherwise. And it is the neutral gear that always creates the difficulty when you are learning to drive.

Whenever you change from one action to another, you come back to the neutral state, to the center. Be aware of it. Someone has insulted you. Now you will change; you cannot remain the same. The periphery will have to change; the same face will not do. The same face has become irrelevant now that someone has insulted you. You will have to change your whole façade. Now be aware of what is happening inside. You will have to go to the center and then come back again to the periphery. Only then can you change your façade. So when someone insults you, meditate on it, go within. He has provided you with a point of change.

Tantra has used intoxicants to make the seeker aware of the changing state of consciousness. They will go on giving you some intoxicant and the teacher will say, "Be aware of the gap." Up to that moment you were aware and now you are losing awareness because of the intoxicant. Be aware of this moment—when you change from consciousness to unconsciousness. When you move from one to the other, be aware. One is always changing and if one can become aware of these changing moments, one becomes aware of the center.

A Zen master will throw you out of the window and will cry from behind, "Be aware!" You have been thrown from the window; you are in between. You are passing through the window, and you are about to hit the ground. He cries, "Be aware!" Once you have fallen on the ground your face must be quite different from what it was before, because now the situation is different.

You may have come to ask some metaphysical question and the master has done something completely nonmetaphysical. You were asking whether God is or not, and he has thrown you out of the window. It is absolutely irrelevant to throw someone through the window. But at the exact moment when you are changing from one state to another, from one face to another, the master says, "Be aware!" When you are passing through the window it is not only your body that is passing through a change; your state of consciousness will be passing through a change. And a teacher knows exactly when it changes. That exact moment he will cry, "Be aware!" And if you can listen to him for that moment, you will be at the center—thrown from the periphery.

So whenever there is any changing situation, be careful to look inside. There is no distance to be traveled: there is only a jump from the periphery to the center and from the center to the periphery. The behavior is just like the behavior of electrons, or just like what happens in dreams. Deepen this awareness. This is all that you can do. It is a negative process, because awareness is not a doing, awareness is not an act.

Whenever you are in a changing state, be aware and there will be no action. Action stops whenever you are aware. If you become aware, then there will not even be any breath. If I put a dagger at your throat, even the breath stops. You become so aware that everything stops. You are thrown to the center. Awareness is not action. In fact, the addiction to action is only an effort to escape from awareness. And we all have become addicted. One must *do* something. This addiction helps you to remain on the periphery.

Use any opportunity to be alert—any opportunity. And there are thousands and thousands of opportunities every day. Be alert and you will feel yourself jump from the periphery to the center. Being at the center can become easy for you. You are outside the house and it has become hot outside. Just come in! Whenever you feel like coming in, you can come in. Whenever you feel like going out, you can go out. There is no difficulty. When the movement from the periphery to the center has become just like this, then you will have an explosion.

I use the word "then," I use the word "slowly"; I say "gradually," I say "by and by." These words are all irrelevant, but because I cannot do anything else, I have to use them. They are irrelevant as far as the explosion is concerned. It is never gradual, it is never slowly, it is never by and by. It is sudden! But you will not be able to understand it, so for your understanding—or, if you like, for your misunderstanding—these words are used.

The whole pattern of language is made for the periphery, so nothing else can be done. Language is created by minds that are on the periphery and it is needed by minds that are on the periphery. It is a necessity of the periphery and not of the center. The center is absolutely silent; no language is needed there. Because we have to interpret what is happening at the center in the language of the periphery, confusion is bound to happen.

So do not misunderstand me when I say "gradually." I never mean gradually; the explosion never comes by and by. These words are only to develop your confidence so that you can hope, so that it can become conceivable for you—so that something may be understood on the periphery. It is just like talking about the world of waking consciousness to a person who is in a dream. One has to use dream language, which is absurd.

Any language is absurd; any expression is absurd in a way. But nothing can be done; one feels completely helpless. And the helplessness is great because one knows something.

For example, I know what is meant by "explosion." I know what is meant by "being at the center." But I cannot tell you. You ask me, I tell you something—and I know all the while that I cannot tell you. I *know* what is meant by "explosion," what is meant by "being at the center," but the moment I begin to speak, I begin to use the language of the periphery. And the moment the language of the periphery is used, everything becomes distorted. So understand these implications.

You ask about chain explosions. Whenever there is an explosion, many things begin to happen. Because the phenomenon is so great, whenever an individual goes through it—wherever he is —he cannot help but become infectious. He may not want it, but this begins to happen. His "being at the center" will push anyone near him to the center also.

Because of this, many times people will begin to feel repuls.

by him. For example, Gurdjieff was felt to be repulsive by many people. They just wanted to run away from him, because by being near him they would be pushed into the unknown. Many women seekers ran away from Gurdjieff because they felt as if they were hit in the sex center just by being near him. They felt he was doing something to them. He was not doing anything, but because our only working center is the sex center, the first impact is always felt there.

Male seekers who came to Gurdjieff did not feel it so much, but women seekers felt it. This is because the physical body of a male has positive bioelectricity and the physical body of a female has negative bioelectricity. The opposite sexes attract each other, so an enlightened man radiates a tremendous energy for female seekers. And both things will happen: women seekers are attracted to a person like Gurdjieff and at the same time repulsed by him.

This inner hit, the inner contact, will be felt in many ways. Each one will feel it in his own way. In the West it is felt very deeply at the sex center for many reasons. One is that the precautions to prevent this from happening are lacking.

In India, a seeker must touch the feet of the guru. It seems unnecessary; it looks like a formality. But there are secret reasons for it. If you bow down to a teacher, if you touch his feet, your sex center will not be hit by his presence. The moment you surrender, his energy will be felt throughout the whole body. A surrendered body becomes whole. You may not have felt this, but now that I have told you about it, you can feel it and know it.

So the Indian way of touching the feet of the guru is to lie down on the earth completely. All parts of the body should touch the earth. We call it *sashtang*, which means that all parts of the body touch the earth when you are lying down on the earth. Then many scientific things begin to happen. Your body becomes a unity and the impact of the guru's presence vibrates on the whole body, not just on one center. It doesn't penetrate a particular center; it penetrates the whole body. You are horizontal and the impact goes through you from the head toward the legs.

If you are vertical, standing, the same impact moves through you, but it cannot go through your whole body, it cannot move to your legs. The only sensitive part of you is the sex center, so the vibration goes to the sex center and doesn't move through the whole body. If you are with a teacher who is living in his center and you are standing, his impact, his vibrations, will pass through your sex center. It may become repulsive to you or it may become attractive, but in either case there will be difficulties. But if you are lying down then the flow passes through you—flowing from one end of you to the other end—and it has a soothing effect.

It took centuries for this inner science to develop in India. What happens is known only through many, many experiences, because man cannot be experimented upon like a guinea pig. It took centuries of observing experiences and happenings to know these things. And as a result of what they have observed, they have made it a basic condition that one must begin with trust, with faith. If you are faithful then you become open; if you are doubting then you are closed. And if you are closed, the same energy that would have helped you toward an explosion will go around and around without being able to penetrate you. So if you are closed, it will not be possible for you to be helped, but if you are open and trusting, the vibration of the master goes deep inside you. Then the explosion becomes a chain explosion. This can happen; this always happens. So a trusting attitude creates chains of explosion.

Sometimes the chain explosion goes on continuously, even after the original teacher has died. For example, in the tradition of the Sikhs, the tenth guru is the last. Until then, one guru was followed by another, but with the tenth the tradition was stopped and broken. What is the reason? Why did Govind Singh stop the chain? It was continuous from Nanak to Govind Singh, it was a living force, but with Govind Singh it was stopped. It could not be delivered and transferred because no one was capable, no one was open to receive it completely, totally. And it cannot be given partially. Either you are totally open, or you are not open at all.

Partial trust is no trust. It is just a deception. Ninety-nine percent of you can't believe—even 99.9 percent will not do. The .1 percent doubt will be enough to kill the whole thing because it will make you closed. But if you trust totally then there is a chain reaction. Then if you come into contact with a master, his touch is not just a touch. It becomes part and parcel of your being.

Really, we are not so isolated as we feel. Our whole sense of isolation is because of the closed attitude of the ego. Otherwise there is no separation, no isolation. You are not so different from me; you are not so separate from me. If you are separate, it is only because of the isolation of the ego. And the miracle of trust is that if you trust, you will not be an ego; and if you doubt, you cannot be other than an ego. If you trust you are not an ego, and then you are no longer isolated.

If you are open to me it does not mean that you are taking anything from me. There is no "me" as such. It is not that you are taking something from someone else; it is only that you see yourself reflected in me. We just look separate from one another because of the ego.

If you are open, the chain of spiritual explosion can continue for centuries. For example, Buddha's chain still continues. Of course, it is not so broad today; it has become a very narrow stream, but it continues.

When Bodhidharma went from India to China it was not to teach someone or to give the message of Buddha to the Chinese and to others. It was only to search for a man who could continue the chain, a man who was so open that before Bodhidharma died he could transfer everything to him.

In China, he sat for nine years, continuously facing a wall. If you went to him, he would not even look at you. His back was toward all visitors. Many people asked, "What is this? Why are you sitting like this?"

Bodhidharma would say, "I have been facing persons for many years, but I have never found in their faces anything other than a wall. No one is receptive; everyone is just like a wall. So it makes no difference now. When you come to me and you are not a wall, I will face you. Only then will I look at you."

For nine years continuously no one came who was capable, no one came whom Bodhidharma could face. Then Hui-Neng came. He stood behind Bodhidharma, cut off his hand and gave it to Bodhidharma, saying, "Now turn around or I will cut off my head!"

Bodhidharma turned around and faced Hui-Neng. He said, "Now the man has come. For you I have traveled across the whole Himalayas." A transmission without scriptures was made. Bodhidharma had no scriptures, so it is said that the transmission was given without scriptures. He just looked in the eyes of Hui-Neng and there was a transmission—from one point to another, with no travel in between.

This, too, must be understood. The chain of explosion is again a jump. When something from my consciousness goes to your consciousness, it is a leap. It was here and now it is there—it was never in between. There is no process. If you are receptive, if you are open, the flame that is here in me will be found in you instantaneously. There will be no time-gap.

The chain can continue forever, but it never does. It is very difficult, because even with a living teacher it is difficult to be open. The mind tries in every way to be closed, because to be open is to die. For the mind it is a death. So the mind will try to be closed. It will argue; it will find many reasons to be closed. It will find very absurd reasons to be closed. Later on, you will not be able to conceive that these things could make you doubt, that these meaningless things made you skeptical. Things that have no meaning at all create the barrier.

But if you are not open, the chain—the transmission—is not possible. All my stress and emphasis on meditation is just to make you open. Any moment you can be open—and there will be a transmission.

Minor explosions happen daily. They are only glimpses of the center. The glimpse is not enough. It can help, but do not be satisfied with it. Ordinarily we become satisfied. There is a glimpse and we become satisfied. We make a treasure out of it and go on remembering it.

When the glimpse has moved from the center to the periphery, it becomes a memory. Then you nourish it, you remember it, you feel elated by it. Then you always wonder when it will happen again. Now it has become part of the periphery, part of the memory. It is useless. These minor explosions can even be harmful if you nourish them as a memory. Throw them, forget them —do not ask for their repetition. Only then will a major explosion be possible, only then will a total explosion be possible.

So there are minor explosions, but I never pay any attention to them. And you should not pay any attention to them either, because a minor explosion becomes part of the memory. It does not destroy the memory. On the contrary, it can strengthen it. So a small experience, a petty experience, cannot do. Throw it! Unless the total is achieved, do not be contented. Before the ultimate explosion happens, do not be satisfied; remain discontented.

Never remember anything that has happened. No experience should be accumulated and nourished. As it happens throw it, forget it, and move on. Nothing short of the total explosion will do, so do not pay any attention to minor explosions.

Things have happened—things are happening—but I never talk about minor explosions. If someone comes to me and says that he has had a minor explosion, I will try to get him to throw it. It should not be remembered or it will become a barrier. You have to continue moving toward the center until you reach a point from which there is no coming back. When that point is reached, it never becomes a part of memory. You remember only things that are lost. That which is always with you, you need not remember.

Really, you become aware of something only when the experience has been lost. If you say, "I love you," be aware that there is every possibility that the love is ending. It may have gone already; it is only an echo of the past. That is why you emphasize, "I love you very much." The "very much" is an effort to fill up the gap. And there is a gap: the love has gone. When love exists, you feel it and live it. Silence is enough. When it is gone, you chatter about it. Now silence is not enough. On the contrary, in silence the dead love will be exposed; in silence you will not be able to hide it. Now you begin to talk about it. Ordinarily you do not speak to reveal things; you speak to hide things. Words are used to hide. In silence you cannot hide anything.

So whenever you become aware of any minor explosion, do not nourish the memory and do not long for its repetition. It has gone; it has become part of the dead past. Throw it! Let the dead be buried and move ahead. And when the real explosion—the major explosion, the ultimate explosion—happens, you will not remember it. You will not need to remember it. It will be with you: it will be your center, it will be your being. You cannot forget it. There is nothing to remember or to forget. And remember, unless the major happens, the minor has no meaning.

You have also asked whether the people who are around me are moving toward the explosion. Yes, they are moving toward it. If they are not moving toward it, they cannot remain with me for long; they cannot continue with me. So whenever those who are incapable come to me, either they leave by themselves or I create situations in which they will go. With them, nothing can be done. I allow those who remain with me, who continue with me, to do so only if they are moving toward the explosion, only if their understanding is deepening, if they are becoming more alert and aware. Of course, the path is arduous and there are many pitfalls. One goes one step ahead and then falls two steps back; it happens daily. The path is not straight; it is crisscrossed. It is not on one plane; it is like a hilly track. So many times you come to the same point—on a slightly higher level.

I allow only those to be near me in whom I see possibilities, potentialities. Otherwise I create situations in which they leave by themselves. And it is very easy to create a situation for someone to leave. It is more difficult to create a situation for someone to stay. Everyone is ready to leave, because to come to the center is the most arduous adventure. And with me, they will always be struggling; they cannot exist on the periphery. Their minds will try every effort in order to remain on the periphery, but they can stay with me only if they are proceeding toward the center.

When you are with me, you continue to be on the periphery and I continue to be at the center. The whole process that happens between you and me is the same as the inner struggle that happens within each one of you. Your being remains at the center and your ego remains on the periphery, so there is struggle and tension. In the same way, when you come to me, you become the periphery and I become the center—and the same struggle begins.

But being with me helps in many ways. If you can continue to be with me for some time, you will be able to remain at your center more easily. The phenomenon that happens between us is the same as it is within each individual. There is no difference. When I talk to you, I talk to you as if you are your center. And when you are with me, it is as if you are your center. One day when you explode into your center you will know that this is so, but before that you cannot know it. Before that you will just have to trust me.

When you come to your center you will know that you have not been living with me; you have been living in your own center's reflection. But you will know that only later on when you pass through it. It will happen; everyone is potentially capable. If you hinder yourself, that is another thing; but otherwise—if you do not hinder yourself, if you are not an enemy to yourself—you are as capable as any Buddha. And the thing will happen. . . .

7

THE ESOTERIC SIGNIFICANCE OF INITIATION

Bhagwan, what does it mean to be initiated into spiritual life? What is the esoteric significance of initiation? Please tell us about the kind of initiation you give to your sannyasins.

Man exists as if in sleep. Man *is* asleep. Whatsoever is known as waking is also a sleep. Initiation means to be in intimate contact with one who is awakened. Unless you are in intimate contact with one who is awakened it is impossible to come out of your sleep, because the mind is even capable of dreaming that it is out of sleep. The mind can dream that now there is no more sleep, but you will not know that it is a dream. You can only know that it was a dream when you are out of it.

You can never know that something is a dream while it is happening. You always become aware of it after it has gone, when it has passed. No one can ever say, "This is a dream"—no present tense can be used for a dream. You can only say that something *was* a dream because, during the dream itself, the dream appears to be real. If a dream does not appear to be real, it will be broken. Only if there is an appearance of reality can a dream be created.

When I say that man is asleep, this has to be understood. We are dreaming continuously, twenty-four hours a day. In the night we are closed to the outer world, dreaming inside. In the day our senses are opened toward the outside world, but the dream continues inside. Close your eyes for a moment and you can again be in a dream. It is a continuity inside. You are aware of the outside world, but that awareness is not without the dreaming mind. It is imposed on the dreaming mind, but inside the dream continues. That is why we are not seeing what is real even when we are supposedly awake. We impose our dreams on reality. We never see what *is;* we always see our projections.

If I look at you and there is a dream in me, you will become an object of projection. I will project my dream on you and whatever I understand about you will be mixed with my dream, my projection. When I love you, you appear to me to be something quite different; when I do not love you, you appear to be completely different. You are not the same because I have just used you as a screen and projected my dreaming mind on you.

When I love you, then the dream is different, so you appear different. When I do not love you, you are the same—the screen is the same—but the projection is different. Now I am using you as a screen for another dream of mine. Then again the dream can change: again I can love you. Then you will appear different to me. We never see what is; we are always seeing our own dreams projected on what is.

The dreaming mind creates a world around it that is not real. That is what is meant by *maya,* illusion. By "illusion" it is not meant that the world is not, that the noise outside on the street is not. It is, but we can never know it *as it is* unless the dreaming mind inside stops. For one person, the noise outside may be music. For someone else, it is just a disturbance. One moment you may not be aware of the noise and the next moment you will become aware of it. In some moments you will tolerate it, in some moments it will become unbearable, intolerable—and the noise is the same, the traffic on the street is the same. But your dreaming mind changes.

As it changes, everything around you takes on a new color.

Thus, when we say the world is illusion, *maya*, it doesn't mean that the world is not. It is, but the way we see it is an illusion. What we see is nowhere to be found.

When someone is awakened, it is not that the real world disappears but only that the world that was known by him before his awakening disappears completely. An altogether new world, an objective world, comes in its place. The coloring, the shape that was given by you, all the meaning and interpretations that were given by you according to your dreaming mind are no more.

As far as this world of *maya*—this world of illusion, this world of projection—is concerned, we never live in one world. Each man lives in his own world, so there are as many worlds as there are dreaming persons. I am not the same to each one of you: each one projects onto me something else. I am one only as far as I am concerned; and if I myself am dreaming, then even for me I am different each moment, because each moment my interpretation will differ.

But if I am awakened, then I am always the same. Buddha has said that the test of an enlightened one is that he is always the same, just like the sea water. Anywhere, everywhere, it is salty. So if I am awakened, then for me I am the same.

Not only in this life. I have been the same in all the lives that have passed, I have been the same for eternity. The real me has remained the same. It is unchangeable. Only the projection changes; the screen remains the same. Only the film changes, the picture changes. But the screen is never seen. You see the picture projected on it. Only when there is no projection do you see the screen; otherwise the screen is never seen. The screen remains the same, but when the picture changes, you see it as a change in me.

If I am awakened, I will remain the same as far as I am concerned, but you will still see me in so many different ways because you will come to me with your dreaming mind, which projects. To someone I may look like a friend and to someone else I may look like an enemy. Each is projecting himself.

We create a world around ourselves, and everyone lives in his own world. That is why there is a collision. Worlds collide: your world and mine. When two persons begin to live in one room there are two worlds living together and collision is inevitable. There are not only two persons living in the room—there are two worlds. The room has enough space for two people, but it does not have enough space for two worlds.

The whole conflict of human society, of human relationship, is a conflict between worlds, not between persons. If I am a person without a world created by my dreams, and you are also a person without a world created by your dreams, we can live in a room for eternity without any collision because the room is big enough for two persons. But for two worlds, even the whole planet is not enough. And there exist many worlds because every individual is a world. He lives inside his own world and is closed to everything outside it.

This is a sort of sleep. You have around yourself a filmy enclosure of projections, ideas, notions, conceptions, interpretations. You are a projector going on and on, projecting things that are nowhere, only inside you, and the whole becomes a screen. So you can never be aware by yourself that you are in deep sleep.

There was a Sufi saint, Hijira. An angel appeared in his dream and told him that he should save as much water as possible from the well because the following morning all the water in the world was going to be poisoned by the devil and everyone who drank it would become mad.

The whole night the fakir saved as much water as possible. And, really, the phenomenon happened! Everyone became mad the next morning. But no one knew the whole city had become mad. Only the fakir was not mad, but the whole city talked as if he had gone mad. He knew what had happened but no one believed him, so he went on drinking his water and remained alone.

But he could not continue that way. The whole city was living in an altogether different world. No one listened to him, and finally there was a rumor that he would be caught and sent to prison. They said that he was mad!

One morning they came to get hold of him. Either he would be treated as if he were ill or he would have to go to prison, but he could not be allowed freedom. He had become absolutely mad! Whatsoever he said could not be understood; he spoke a different language.

The fakir was at a loss to understand. He tried to help the others to remember their past, but they had forgotten everything. They did not know anything of the past, anything about what had existed before that maddening morning. They could not understand. The fakir had become incomprehensible to them.

They surrounded his house and caught hold of him. Then the fakir said, "Give me one minute more. I shall cure myself." He ran to the common well, drank the water, and became all right. The whole city was happy: the fakir was okay; now he was not mad. Really, he had gone mad now, but he was part and parcel of the common world.

So if everyone is asleep, you will never even be aware that you are asleep. If everyone is mad and you are mad, you will never be aware of it.

By "initiation" it is meant that you have surrendered to someone who is awakened. You say, "I do not understand; I cannot understand. I am part and parcel of the world that is mad and asleep; I am dreaming all the time. My reasoning is phony because whenever I act, I act from the irrational part of the mind. I always act unconsciously, and then later on I rationalize it. I fall in love with someone and then I begin to rationalize why I love, what the reason for it is. The phenomenon happens this way: first I begin to like something and then I find reasons why I like it. The liking comes first, then the rationalization follows. And the liking is irrational!"

This feeling can come even from a sleepy person, because the sleep is not always deep. It wavers, becoming very deep at times and then becoming very shallow. Sleep is never on one plane. Even in ordinary sleep there are fluctuations; sleep is not the same the whole night.

Sometimes the sleep is so deep that you cannot remember

anything about it later on. If you have slept very deeply, then in the morning you say, "I have not dreamed anything." You *have* dreamed, but the sleep was so deep that you cannot remember. There are scientific implements that can show that you have dreamed, but you will deny it because there is no memory of it. You were sleeping so deeply, you were so far away from your conscious mind, that the mind could not pick up anything from the dream.

Other times your sleep is very shallow, just on the border of waking. Then you can remember your dream. Ordinarily we remember only the dreams we have in the morning just before we come out of sleep, because the sleep is very shallow then and the gap between the conscious mind and the unconscious mind is very small.

Ordinary sleep is a fluctuation of many levels, many planes. Sometimes you are wavering between waking and sleep. When you are wavering, you can hear something that is happening outside the dream. You have gone to sleep. You hear something: someone is talking about something. Part of it is understood and part of it is lost, but you can hear it. Another time, when you are fast asleep, in a deep sleep, someone may be talking but you cannot hear it. There is no question of interpretation, there is no question of meaning—you simply cannot hear it.

The same thing that happens in ordinary sleep happens in the metaphysical sleep that I am talking about. Sometimes you are just on the border line, very near to the Buddha. Then you can understand something of what Buddha is saying. Of course, it will never be exactly what was said, but at least you have heard something, at least you have a glimpse of the truth.

So a person who is on the border of metaphysical sleep will want to be initiated. He can hear something, he can understand something, he sees something. Everything is as if in a mist, but still he feels something. Now he can approach a person who is awakened and surrender himself. This much can be done by a sleepy person: he can surrender. This surrendering means he understands that something quite different from his sleep is hap-

pening. Somewhere he feels it. He cannot know what it is, but
he feels it.

Whenever a Buddha passes, those who are on the border line
of sleep can recognize something different about this man. He
behaves differently, he speaks differently, he lives differently, he
walks differently. Something has happened to him. Those who are
on the border line can feel it. But they are asleep, and this
borderline awareness is not permanent. They may fall back into
sleep again at any moment. Or, even a word can pull them out.

Before they fall into a deeper unconsciousness, they can surrender to an awakened one. This is initiation from the side of the
initiated. He says, "I cannot do anything myself; I am helpless.
I know that if I do not surrender this moment, I may again go
into deep sleep. Then it will be impossible to surrender." So there
are moments that should not be lost, and one who loses those
moments may not be able to get them again for centuries, for
lifetimes, because it is not in one's hands when one will again
come to the border line. It happens for many reasons that are
beyond your control. You cannot control your sleep.

Sometimes it happens that Buddha, or someone like Buddha,
is passing. You can surrender, but only if you are on the border.
There is a very meaningful story in Buddha's life. When he
himself became awakened, he was silent for ten days continuously. He did not feel like speaking. This is a very beautiful story.
The gods became uneasy, because if Buddha remained silent,
what would become of those who were on the border line? He
could not do anything for those who were in deep sleep—even a
Buddha cannot do anything for them!—and he could not do
anything for those who were already awakened (they do not need
any help from him), but there were a few who were just on the
edge. Just a small push would awaken them; his very presence
might be enough to awaken them.

So the gods came to Buddha, prayed to him, and asked him to
speak. Buddha said to them, "There are persons who cannot be
helped. They are so fast asleep that it is useless to speak to them.
And those who can listen to me are already awake, so there is no

need to talk to them either. Why do you ask me to talk? It is meaningless. Let me remain silent."

The gods said, "But there is still a category that is left: those who are not fast asleep but who are not so awake that they can understand. They are just on the border. They may not even listen to all you say, but just a word may pull them out of their sleep. You must speak. It is only after thousands and thousands of years that a person becomes a Buddha. He must speak; he must not remain silent. The opportunity must not be lost."

Buddha became convinced. Yes, there is a third category. That category is the category of the initiates.

From the one who is being initiated, nothing but surrender will do. Initiation means to be surrendered. The Buddhist term for initiation, for one who is being initiated, is *shrotapann,* one who has entered the current. Buddha is flowing just like a current. One who surrenders himself, who enters the current and begins flowing, is *shrotapann.* The current cannot come to you, but it is flowing by the side of your house. You can jump into it.

But if you jump into the current and try to swim, you will begin to resist, to fight with the current. You will have your own aims, your own goals to reach somewhere. There are persons who come to an enlightened one and begin to argue. They want reasons, they ask for proofs, they would like to be convinced. It is a struggle: they are fighting with the master. This does not harm the master but it harms the one who is struggling, because the moment is being lost. He was on the border line—that is why he has come—but now he is missing the moment. And it may be that he will again go into deep sleep.

Surrendering means one who begins to flow with the stream, who gives himself up to the stream. Now the stream flows; he follows it. He is just in a let-go, a total let-go. On the part of the initiated, initiation is a let-go: a complete trust, a total surrender.

It can never be partial. If you surrender partially, you are not surrendering. You are deceiving yourself. There can be no partial surrender, because in a partial surrender you are withholding something, and that withholding may push you again into a deep sleep. That nonsurrendering part will prove fatal. Any moment you may again be in deep sleep.

Surrender is always total. That is why faith was required, and always will be required, in initiation. Faith is required as a total condition, as a total requirement. And the moment you surrender totally, things begin to change. Now you cannot go back to your dream-life. This surrendering shatters the whole projection, this surrendering shatters the whole projecting mind, because the projecting mind is tethered to the ego; it cannot live without the ego. The ego is the main center of it, the base.

I call someone my friend—why? I call someone my enemy— why? An enemy is one who has hurt my ego and a friend is one who has fed it, who has nourished it. That is why we say that in times of need you know who your friends are. "A friend in need is a friend indeed." What is this need? The need comes when your ego is starving. Then you know who your friends are.

Our whole dreaming world, our dreaming mind, rests on the pedestal of the ego. If you have surrendered, you have surrendered the very base. You have given up completely. Now you cannot continue wavering, because the dream itself has been given up.

So from the side of the initiate, initiation is a total surrender. But what is it on the part of the one who initiates you? As far as the initiated one is concerned, it is not very difficult to understand what initiation is. It is very simple. It is just a person who is asleep asking for help to be awakened. He surrenders to someone who is awake. It is very simple. But for the one who initiates you, the thing is very complex, very difficult.

Ordinarily, we think that surrendering is very difficult. But you are helpless; in the end you will not be able to do anything else. You may not surrender right away, but when you know more, you will come to the point of surrendering. One day it is bound to come because you cannot do anything else. You cannot continue with a nonsurrendering attitude because this will create miseries, agony, and hell for you. You cannot continue. There is bound to come one moment when, out of your own frustration, out of your own nightmare, you will surrender.

This is not the difficult part of initiation; this is a very simple thing. But for the one who initiates you, it is a very complex affair. There are many things involved and many of these things are esoteric, not exoteric. First, we will have to understand the exoteric, the outer things, and then we can proceed to the esoteric, the inner things.

The first thing. Corresponding to surrender is responsibility. The one who is asleep surrenders; the one who is awake takes the responsibility. When you go to a Buddha, to a Jesus, to a Mohammed, and surrender yourself, he takes the whole responsibility. What you are surrendering is your sleep, your dreams. You cannot surrender anything more because you *are* nothing more than sleep and dreams. You surrender this—your sleep, your dreaming, your whole nonsense of the past.

Surrendering is always of the past and responsibility is always for the future. You yourself have no future, you are only the dreamy past. A long number of memories, the dreams of many lives, is surrendered. And that, too, you surrender with difficulty. It is arduous to surrender even this dusty past. But you have nothing else: you have been asleep the whole time and dreaming. You have a record of many dreams—good or bad, beautiful or ugly—but dreams all the same. When the opportunity is there, you surrender your dreams before you are lost again in them. But that, too, is a great hardship; that, too, is very difficult. It is a struggle. You try to withhold, to resist—something must be saved! But what have you got? Nothing but a long series of dreams, a long sleep.

So from the initiated, it is a surrendering of the past; and from the one who initiates you, it is a responsibility for the future. He becomes responsible for you. And only he *can* be responsible; you can never be responsible. How can one who is asleep be responsible? Responsibility is never a part of sleep.

If you commit a murder in your sleep—if you are a somnambulist walking in your sleep and you commit a murder—no court will hold you responsible because you can never be responsible in a dream. How can a person who is in a deep sleep be responsible? You never feel responsible for your dreams: you can do anything in your dreams but you never feel any responsibility. You can even murder, but you will say that it was just a dream. Responsibility comes with awakening.

This is really a fundamental law of life: one who is asleep is not responsible even for himself, and one who is awakened is responsible even for others. A person who is enlightened, who is awakened, feels he is responsible for the whole mess you have created. A Buddha feels compassion; he feels guilty for your crimes, for your sins. He feels involved; he feels responsible. He knows that you do not know what you are doing, but he is fully aware of it.

For example, a third world war is going to happen. One who is awakened knows fully well that it is coming. Every day it comes closer; soon it will be here. You are deep in sleep, but he is not asleep, he is not dreaming. He is fully conscious, like radar. He knows what future is coming. He feels guilty; he feels he must do something. It is like when you are in a plane, flying in the sky. You are asleep, dreaming, but the pilot is aware. If anything is going to happen, only he will be responsible; no one else is responsible. He is fully awake, and he is the only one who is.

So a Buddha will feel responsible for all our crimes and sins. The whole story of Jesus is based on this responsibility; the whole of Christianity, the whole concept, begins from this responsibility. Jesus feels responsible for the whole sin of man from Adam up to us. Jesus feels responsible. He takes the cross on his shoulders in order that our sins may be pardoned, forgiven.

Jesus is in no way responsible. If Adam has done something, if the whole human mind has done something, why should he be responsible? Christian theologians have discussed this for centuries. He has not committed any sins. Still, he feels responsible because he is awakened. By the very phenomenon of being awakened, he has become responsible for everything that the sleeping ones have done. His burden has grown; his cross is heavy. His crucifixion is symbolic: he dies for us so that we may live.

That is why the crucifixion of Jesus has become a historic date. He is a person who feels responsible for the whole human race and dies for it so that man may be transformed. But even with his death we are not transformed. His message is heard in our dreams and we interpret it in our own ways. Then his life becomes a part of our dreaming world. Then we create churches and dogmas, then we create sects. Then there are Catholic and Protestant sects and so many others. The whole nonsense continues in many new ways, and the world remains the same.

We begin to worship him. That is, we begin to dream about him—that he is the son of God. We are not surrendered, we are not transformed. Rather, on the contrary, we transform his reality into our dreams. We create a church for him; we make an idol of him. We worship him and continue our sleep. Really, we use him as a tranquilizer.

It becomes a Sunday affair. For one hour a week we go to him and then we continue in our own way. He helps us to sleep well: our conscience becomes easy; we feel religious. We go to church to pray, to worship, and come back home the same as we were. But now we are less uneasy. Now there is no burden to be religious, to be transformed. We are already religious because we have been to church where we have worshiped and prayed. We are religious already! And the whole thing continues in the same way.

Corresponding to surrendering is responsibility. Responsibility means answerability. It means Jesus feels answerable for you. He feels that if there is any God, he will be responsible for you before God. He will be asked, and he will have to answer why this or that happened to humanity. Responsibility means this. It is something that happens naturally with him.

But if you come to him and surrender to him, then he becomes particularly responsible for you. So Krishna could say to Arjuna, "Leave everything. Come to me; surrender at my feet," and Jesus could say, "I am the truth, I am the door, I am the gate. Come to me, pass through me. I will be the witness on the last day of your judgment. I will answer for you."

This is analogical. Every day is the day of judgment, and every moment is the moment of judgment. There is not going to be any last day. These are just terms that could be understood by the people to whom Jesus was speaking. Really, he was saying, "I will be responsible for you and I will answer for you when the divine asks. I will be there as a witness. Surrender to me. I will be your witness."

This is a great responsibility. No one who is asleep can take it because even to be responsible for yourself becomes difficult in sleep. You cannot be responsible for others if you are asleep. You can be responsible for others only when you no longer need to be responsible for yourself, when you are unburdened completely—really, when you are no more.

This declaration of being "no more" has been made in many ways. When Jesus said, "I am the son of my Father who is in heaven," what he meant is that he is not the son of the person who is known as his father, he is not the son of Mary who is known as his mother.

Why does he say this? Sometimes it seems very cruel. One day he was standing in a crowd and someone said, "Your mother, Mary, has come. She is outside the crowd and she is waiting for you."

Jesus said, "I have no mother. Who is my mother? Who is my father? No one is my mother, no one is my father." It appears cruel. The mother is standing outside the crowd, she is waiting, and Jesus says to tell her that "No one is my mother and no one is my father." Why?

He is just denying the pattern of your dreams: this is my father, my mother, my wife, my brother. This is the pattern of the dreaming mind—the dreaming world, the world of projection. He simply denies it. The moment you have denied the mother you have denied the whole world, because with her the whole world begins. That is the beginning: the root from where you have come into this dreaming world—the root of relationship, of *sansar*.

If you deny your mother you have denied everything. It appears cruel to those who are fast asleep, but it is simply a fact. To emphasize that "I am the son of the one who is in heaven" is just to say that "I am not an individual. I am not Jesus, the son of Mary. I am part and parcel of the divine force, the cosmic force."

Only one who feels like that—who feels like part of the cosmic —can initiate you. Otherwise no one can initiate you. No particular individual can initiate you, and if that happens (and it happens so many times, it is happening every day—those who are themselves asleep initiate others who are asleep: the blind leading the blind), then both fall into the ditch.

No one who is asleep can initiate anyone, but the ego wants to initiate. This egoistic attitude has proved fatal and very dangerous. The whole concept of initiation, the whole mystery of it, the whole beauty of it, became ugly because of those who were not entitled to initiate. Only one who has no ego inside, who has no sleep inside, who has no dream inside, can initiate. Otherwise, initiation is the greatest sin, because you are not only deceiving others but yourself also. Initiation is a great responsibility, the ultimate responsibility. Now you are becoming responsible for another. And to become responsible for someone is not just a game. It is taking the impossible in your hands: you are becoming responsible for someone in their folly.

This responsibility can be taken only when there is a total surrender. Otherwise it cannot be taken. Responsibility cannot be taken for one who is withholding himself, because he will continue in his own way, he will not listen to you. He will interpret you in his own ways.

There is a Sufi story. A rich man died. He was not only rich, he was also wise, which happens very rarely. His son was only ten or twelve years of age, so he had made a will which was given to the elders of the village, the *panchayat*. In the will he proclaimed to the elders: "Take from my property whatever you like most and then give to my child."

The will was as clear as day, so the five elders divided the man's whole property. Everything that was of any worth they divided between themselves until nothing was left except a little bit that was useless. No one wanted to take it, so it was given to the child.

But the dying old man had also given a letter to the boy, which he was to open when he became of age. When he was of age, he opened the letter, in which his father had written: "What I meant by the will they may, of course, interpret in their own way. When you become of age, give it this interpretation. This is my interpretation. This is what I meant to say." Then these instructions were written: "Take all that you like most and then, all that you like most—give it to my child."

The son produced the letter before the elders. They had never conceived of such a meaning so they had divided everything among themselves. Now they had to return the whole thing because the meaning of it was clear. And now the boy was ready.

The father had also written in the note: "It is good that the elders should interpret in their own way until the time comes for you to take it. If I give it to you directly, before you are of age, it will be destroyed by the elders. So let them protect it as their own property until you are ready to take it over." And they had protected it, as he knew they would, because it was theirs.

So whenever there is a partial surrender, you will interpret any message, any commandment, any order to you by the part that appeals to you most. You are sleeping, so any meaning you give to it will come through your sleeping mind. So unless one surrenders totally, the responsibility cannot be taken. But when one surrenders totally, the total responsibility goes to the teacher, to the awakened one. Your surrender is total, his responsibility is total.

In the old days, to take initiation was not easy. It was the most difficult thing. The very phenomenon was such that it *had* to be difficult. One had to wait for years to be initiated. Even for his whole life one might wait, because unless he was ready he could not be initiated.

This waiting stage was really a testing ground. Are you patient? Can you wait? Only in waiting is your maturity revealed. A child cannot wait even for a single moment: if he wants a toy he wants it right now; he cannot wait. The more impatient the mind, the less mature.

In the old days, before initiation could happen, one had to wait for many years. This waiting was a testing ground. It was also a discipline. For example, Sufis would initiate you only when you had waited for a particular period. You had to wait without questioning for the moment when the teacher himself would say that it was time.

Meanwhile, one would do many things. For example, a Sufi might be a shoemaker. If you wanted to be initiated, you would have to help him for years in shoemaking. And not even the relevance of the shoemaking could be questioned. You could not ask what would happen by the shoemaking, how it would help to make you self-realized, how you would become divine through it. You could not ask the relevance of the shoemaking. If even the relevance was asked about, you would be thrown out because it is not your business. To know what is relevant is the teacher's business. How can you know? You do not know the divine, so you cannot know how shoemaking is related to the divine. You cannot know.

For five years you would be just waiting, helping the teacher in shoemaking. He would never talk of prayer or meditation, he would never talk of anything except shoemaking. You would wait like this for five years. But this is a meditation! And it is no ordinary meditation—you would be cleansed through it. This simple waiting, this unquestioned waiting, this relying totally on the master, would make the ground ready for a complete surrender.

Sometimes it looks so easy from the outside. It is not easy; it is very difficult. Your mind will resist, your mind will ask questions, your mind will raise problems. It will ask, "What are you doing? Are you doing the right thing or are you just wasting your time? Is this man with his shoemaking really worth being with? Is it in any way related to the search?"

The mind will continue to ask. Inside you will be bubbling, and yet you cannot ask. You have to rely on the master; you have to wait for the right moment. But if you can wait for even one year, the mind will become silent by itself. It cannot continue unless you feed it daily, unless you help it daily. Unless you become daily perturbed by it, daily disturbed by it, it cannot continue. You have just been waiting while the mind goes on chattering and raising questions. You have waited and waited and waited until finally all questions become meaningless. Finally, the mind will be exhausted. It will lose interest; it will just go dead. You go on waiting and a moment comes when there is no questioning.

When there is no questioning, then the teacher will answer. Exactly the moment there is no questioning within the disciple is the moment for the teacher to answer, because now you can hear. Your chattering has stopped. Now you are silent, now you have become a passage.

Ordinarily, we feed the mind continually. We cannot even wait for an hour to see whether the mind will continue if we do not go on feeding it. It cannot continue because there is nothing permanent about it. If it is not continually replenished, it will go by itself.

A Tibetan teacher, Milarepa, had it as a rule that if you wanted to ask him a question you could ask it only after you had waited for seven days. This is the price one had to pay—and one has to pay a price for everything. If you asked right away, he would throw you out. He would say, "Wait for seven days. Stay with the question." But you cannot stay with a question for seven days. Seven days is too long.

Sometimes someone comes to me and asks me a question. If I can dodge the question and talk about something else for even two minutes, he forgets the question; he never comes back to it again. He can talk for an hour and will not come back to the question again. It was just a whim, just a wave; it means nothing.

So if you can wait for five years you will not be the same. But waiting will be very difficult. In the old days initiation was done after a long wait, but then surrender was easy and total responsibility for the disciple could be taken.

Now the whole thing has become different because no one is ready to wait. The most acute disease of the modern mind is hurry. Time consciousness is the new phenomenon of the modern mind; the basic change that has happened in the mind is time consciousness. We have become so time conscious that we cannot wait for even a single moment. It is impossible. That is why the whole age has become childish. There is no maturity anywhere because maturity is always a by-product of waiting, and waiting is possible only with timeless consciousness, not with time consciousness.

Because of this time consciousness, initiation has become impossible. You cannot be initiated. You run past Buddha and you ask him, "Will you initiate me?" You are running; you meet Buddha on the street while you are running. Even during this utterance of four or five words you have been running. So maturity has become impossible.

But why is this time consciousness, which is the greatest barrier, there? Why was it not there before and why is it so pronounced now?

Time consciousness deepens when you become afraid of death. You may not be aware of it, but the more you become aware of death, the more you become time conscious. Not even a single moment should be lost because death is there. Every moment that is lost is lost forever, and death comes nearer and nearer. You are going to die, so you have to use every moment. You cannot wait, because waiting only means death. Death is coming! No one can wait; no one knows what is going to happen tomorrow. The next moment, death may come. You become uneasy. You begin trembling, you begin to run.

This whole hurrying of the modern mind is because of the fear of death. For the first time man is so afraid of death because for the first time man has become absolutely unaware of the deathless. If you are aware of the deathless, then there is no hurry. You live in eternity and there is always enough time—more than enough, always enough. Nothing is lost, because time is eternal. It is not that if you waste a moment, less time will be left. Time remains the same because it is eternal. From a treasury that is immeasurable you cannot lose anything. Even if you go on losing, it makes no difference; the remainder remains the same. You cannot take anything away from it.

But we think that time is short and death will soon be there because we are only conscious of the body, which is going to die. We are not conscious of the inner consciousness, which is deathless. In ancient days there were people who were conscious of the deathless and, because of their consciousness, their deathlessness, they created an atmosphere in which there was no hurry. Things would move slowly if they moved at all. Then initiation was easy, then waiting was easy, then surrender was easy. Then for the master to assume responsibility for the disciple was easy.

These things have all become difficult now, but there is still no alternative. Initiation is needed! The old initiation has become impossible, so a new initiation must replace it. The old initiation must be replaced by a newer one. My whole effort is toward that.

If you are in a hurry, then I will give initiation to you in your running state of affairs, because otherwise there will be no initiation. I cannot ask you to wait as a precondition. I must initiate you first and then prolong your waiting in many ways. Through many devices I will persuade you to wait, because without waiting there is no maturity. Then when you are ready, there will be a second initiation, which would have been the first in the old days but cannot be the first now.

Sometimes people are bewildered by it. Sometimes when someone comes to me, he has not even heard about me before, he has not known anything about me, and I initiate him into *sannyas*. This is absurd, not understandable at all. But I know why I am doing it. Whatever I am doing, I am doing very considerately. This initiation is just the beginning, because only through this initiation will I be able to create devices for his waiting. He cannot just wait. If I tell him to wait for five years and then I will initiate him, he will not be able to wait. But if I give *sannyas* to him this very moment, he will be able to wait.

So let it be like this; it makes no difference. The process will be the same. Because you cannot wait, I change. I will allow you to wait afterward and then there will be a second initiation. The first initiation is a formal one; the second one will be informal. It will be like a happening. You will not ask me for it; I will not give it to you. It will happen. In the innermost being, it will happen. And you will know it when it happens.

There is no other way possible in the world at this moment. For the time-conscious mind, there is no other way. So first I will push you and then I will work on you. And the working is also going to be quite different; it cannot be the same.

For example, I will have to work much with your intellect, which was never needed before. It was always thought of as a barrier. I also know that it is a barrier, I am also aware that nothing can really happen with the intellect; but I will have to work and labor with your intellect. If I say that your intellect is not needed, this statement will be interpreted by your intellect and you will feel disconnected from me. Then there will be no further intimacy; the door between us will be closed. So this cannot be said today. Of course, it is a basic truth, but it cannot be uttered as it was uttered in the old days.

Now I will have to do much with your intellect. And only when I have worked with your intellect so much, in a way never before worked with it—more than your capacity—only then will you be ready for the statement "Throw the intellect!"—not before. You become convinced, and intellect becomes convinced very easily because it is a very superficial part. Only if you become convinced that what I have said is rational can I begin to work with the irrational. That is the real beginning, but to come to your heart I will have to go around and around, through your intellectual bypasses. The labyrinth of intellect has to be unnecessarily traveled. But for this age it has become necessary. Now even the irrational will have to be approached through rational effort.

This period of waiting will train the intellect to look toward the beyond. And simultaneously I will force you, push you, toward meditation. In the old days meditation was very secret, very esoteric. It would be given to you only when you were totally ready, because it is the most secret key of the most secret treasure. It can be given only when you are completely ready; otherwise it cannot be given. But if I wait for your readiness, it is not going to be given to you at all. So I will give you a key. Of course, a false one. You can toy with it, and you can wait. More than the key, the waiting will help.

Even with a false key you will be more at ease. And the key is made in such a way that if you go on using it, it will become authentic. The key is made in such a way that you go on trying it, but it cannot unlock the door this very moment. Right now the key is false: it has corners, which it should not have. But if you go on trying with it, those corners will disappear; they will wither away. It will become a real key. Daily, it will move more and more freely. I think you understand me. I am not going to replace a false key with another key. The same key will become authentic by repeated use! The unnecessary corners of it will wither away.

I cannot wait for you to be ready to be given a key that can open the door this very moment. The door is ready, the key is ready, but you are not ready. So there are two ways. The old way is that you should wait. I will say, "Wait five years. This is the key, that is the door, but wait for five years. Do not ask again where the key is; do not even touch the door in curiosity, do not go near the lock. Wait!" And if I see that you are even looking at the lock, I will send you away. You are just to wait: never to look at the lock, never to be greedy for it. "This is the key. I will give it to you when you are ready."

This is the old way. People waited for years; even for lives people have waited. There is a story.

One disciple waited for three lives. The teacher was experimenting with him to see how much he could wait. He said, "I want to know how much you can wait."

The disciple said, "Okay, I will also see how much *you* can wait."

It is going to be a waiting for both. Never think that it is going to be a waiting for you alone. If you are waiting, I am also waiting.

And I am in more of a hurry than you, because I may not be here again.

So the disciple said, "Let us see who can wait longer."

It became difficult for the teacher. He had to come again for three lives, and the disciple was still waiting. Each time he would sit and wait, and each time the same story was repeated. In the end, the teacher lost patience. He said, "Take this key, finally. You have won! I am defeated."

The disciple said, "Why are you in such a hurry? I can wait still longer."

The teacher said, *"You* can wait, but I have to come back to earth unnecessarily each time just for this waiting. It looks as if you can continue forever. So take the key!"

But the disciple said, "The key has already come to me because such long waiting has itself become a key. Now I do not need it."

The teacher said, "That is another reason why I was in such a hurry. I knew that if you waited even longer, there would be no need for the key to be given. The very waiting would become a key."

This was the old way. Wait first—then the key will be given. But now that is not possible, so I have to change the whole thing. First I give you the key. Then you can play with it. You cannot wait unoccupied, but you can wait occupied. Now you have the key, you have the lock. The door is there, you have heard rumors about the treasure—you have everything.

I go on creating rumors about the treasure. You have the key so you can wait. You can play with the lock and key. And by this very playing and waiting, the false key will turn into an authentic one.

Responsibility from the teacher corresponds to the surrender of the disciple. There are many other things that the teacher does that have no correspondence within the disciple. Only in one thing is there a correspondence between what the teacher does and what the disciple does. This is the bridge: surrender from the disciple and responsibility from the teacher.

There are many things that are the concern of only the teacher. Really, the disciple does not have to do much; the teacher has to do much. And that is right, that is how it should be. But the disciple always thinks that he is doing much.

The teacher has to do so much, so many things. He can only indicate some of this. He has to work with you on many layers simultaneously.

First, he has to work with your body. You cannot understand what he is doing because you are completely unaware of your body. You do not know anything about your body. You only know your body when you feel hungry, when you feel pain, disease; that is all. That is your only contact with your body; you do not know what a great phenomenon your body is.

The teacher has to do much with your body because, unless your body is transformed, the innermost part of you cannot be tackled. And he has to do this in such a way that you do not become aware that he is doing something with your body. If you become aware of it, this very consciousness will create a disturbance in your body and the teacher will not be able to do his work. This is a secret phenomenon of the body: it works when you are not conscious of it, but if you become conscious of it, it will not work.

For example, you can do an experiment tomorrow. Be conscious while you are eating, and then be conscious of the stomach working to change the food into living nourishment. Be conscious of this process for twenty-four hours and you will feel sick; your stomach will be disturbed. You will not be able to be nourished by the food. It will become poison; you will have to throw it completely. The whole system will be disturbed.

That is why you need sleep. During sleep the body can function better because you are not conscious. So if someone is ill, the doctor will first find out whether his sleep is good. If he is not sleeping, no medicine will do, no help can be given. He cannot be helped because his body cannot work—he is too conscious of it.

Many diseases continue unnecessarily because of this consciousness. Once your stomach is disturbed, you become conscious about it. Then the stomach becomes all right, but the consciousness of it continues. Now this consciousness will disturb your stomach more and it will become a vicious circle. Your consciousness is disturbed by your stomach and your stomach is disturbed by your consciousness. You cannot finish with it. It will continue; it will become a lifelong condition.

One day your sleep is disturbed. The next day you are all right, but now you have become conscious of sleep. You think that it may be that sleep will also not come today. You have become conscious of sleep, so it will not come. You are too conscious of it. Then the next day you will be even more conscious of it.

So the teacher has to do many things with your body that he cannot tell you about. Even a touch will be doing something; even a hand on your head will be doing something. In the old world, with ancient people, it was very easy because they were not so body conscious. But with time consciousness there is a corresponding corollary of body consciousness. I call it "death consciousness." Really, the more you are death conscious, the more you will be body conscious.

Today, everyone has become so body conscious that you cannot touch someone without his becoming self-conscious. But the moment he becomes self-conscious, the inner meaning of the master's touch, the inner working of it, stops.

We have become so afraid of touch—so touchy. Everyone is constantly aware that no one should touch him. You are standing in a crowd and everyone is touching, but somewhere inside you are trying all the while not to be touched. So things have become difficult in this way, unnecessarily difficult.

Now I have to create many different devices in which your body can be changed. In my method of Dynamic Meditation I have added a cathartic part only in order to change your body center. No old meditation technique had this part added because catharsis could be brought about by the teacher. His touch—just a single touch on any one of your centers—could bring up so much catharsis. But now that is very difficult.

For example, a Zen teacher will have a staff in his hand and he will beat the disciple with his staff. No Westerner can understand what the meaning of it is—not even those who are sympathetic. And a Zen teacher will not tell what is meant by it. It is not just a beating; it is a hammering on a particular center. It is not a beating at all. But what the teacher is doing has to be hidden. For example, he is beating on your backbone, on a particular part. If he says to you, "I am touching a certain center in order to help your body to work in a particular way," you will become self-conscious of it. So he will not say that. He will say, "I feel that you are sleepy, so I am beating you," and whenever you feel sleepy, he will come and beat you.

This beating is a hidden trick to camouflage the whole affair. You will think, "He is beating me," and you will not become aware of the center that he has hammered. But now, this too cannot be done.

Asanas have been used to change your inner flow, *mudras* have been used, but these have to be practiced a long time. No one can practice for so long now. And they have to be practiced in a very isolated atmosphere, not in the marketplace. When you practice particular *asanas* and *mudras,* and the practice goes deep, the particular centers that are worked on become so sensitive that you must remain isolated or many unnecessary disturbances will be there. When your centers become open, you become very sensitive and an isolated atmosphere is needed.

So a teacher has to do much with your body, through so many methods. It is always up to him to devise new methods, because old methods become useless. The more you know, the more self-conscious you become, so new methods have to be created continually.

Only an enlightened master can create new methods. Those who are initiating disciples and are not enlightened themselves will have to rely on old methods because they cannot devise new ones. They do not even know what is meant by the techniques they teach; they know only the outer gestures. So they will continue to use hatha yoga, *pranayama*—they will continue. Wi every new enlightened person, the world gets new devices; otherwise it cannot get new devices. And each new age needs new devices because in each new age the mind is different.

The teacher has to do so much with your body—that is the beginning. And the difficult part of it is that you must not be aware of it. That is why it is meaningful to live with the teacher: to live in an ashram, to sleep with a teacher. Then, without your knowing it, your body is more vulnerable for his work to happen.

Teachers have even used intoxicants to make you unconscious so that they can work with your body. Anesthetics are used not only by surgeons; teachers have also used them in their own way. When you are completely unaware, then they can work. And the work that cannot ordinarily be done in a year can be done in a moment then, because the exact point can be touched, turned, changed, and the whole direction of your energy can be made different.

Things become even more difficult because the energy that is to be worked with lies at the sex center. This makes it even more difficult. It, too, is part of the whole complexity.

I am talking about time consciousness, death consciousness, and sex consciousness. They are all parts of one thing. The more you become death conscious, the more you will feel sexual, because sex is the antidote to life. Sex is the beginning of life and death is the end. If you are more conscious of death, you will become more conscious of sex.

Only a society that is not conscious of death will be unconscious of sex. That does not mean that it will not be sexual, but only that it will be unconscious of it. Sex will just be a natural thing. If you go to a primitive society and touch the breast of a woman and ask her what it is, she will reply in an automatic way —with no reference to morality, with no reference to body consciousness, with no reference to sex. She will simply say, "This is to give milk to the child."

Our energy lies in the sex center. And we have become so conscious of the sex center, we guard it so continuously, we have become so tense about it, that it goes on becoming more and more difficult to help. That is why I have created many new devices and why I talk about different things from many dimensions. For example, I have talked about "from sex to superconsciousness" so much only to relax you. If you can become relaxed at your sex center, if there is no tension, then the energy can be released upward.

So the first thing the teacher has to do is to help your body to change. It has to be changed because a new phenomenon is going to happen to your body. It has to be prepared for the new explosion that is going to come, that is going to descend, for the new energy that will soon be your guest. You have to be made a host, so the whole arrangement has to be changed.

The arrangement—as we exist ordinarily—will not do. It is a biological arrangement. The whole structure of the body, the whole pattern of the body, is biological. It is used only as a sex vehicle. The whole process of the body is just to perpetuate itself. Nothing more is expected from your body as far as nature is concerned, so the whole pattern of the body is arranged in that way. But now you do not only want to continue the race. You want to change the whole biological process to create a new dimension: absolutely nonbiological—spiritual. The whole structure of the body has to be changed.

So the teacher has to work much with your body and then much with your emotions. And now—even much with your intellect. All this is the conscious, the exoteric work.

The teacher has to do many things to the outer parts of you in initiation. But there is also the inner part, the esoteric. The teacher works on the inner parts through telepathic messages, through your dreams, through visions, through secret communications. Your intellect can be pacified directly—it can be talked to and pacified; it can be argued with and pacified directly—but not your emotions. One has to work directly with your emotions. One has to create milieus through which your emotions are changed, transformed.

But that, too, is outer. Your emotions, your intellect, your body

—these are the outer shells of your being. You reside within; your being is deeper inside. That being also has to be transformed. This is done through telepathic means, through esoteric, secret paths.

Your dreams can be used—they are used. In fact, it often happens that you may not be aware of your dreams but your teacher is. And he is more interested in your dreams than in your waking state. Your so-called waking consciousness is false; it is not real. You are not expressed in it; you are only acting. Your dreams are more real.

Freud used dream analysis because of some alchemical tradition that became known to him. Something from some esoteric circle leaked out. He used it and created a whole science out of it. Of course, he could not know your dreams directly. He had to make you confess, to make you show him your dream, remember your dream, talk about your dream. Then he could analyze it. But in initiation, the teacher knows your dreams. He can go into your dreams, he can be a witness to your dreams. Then he knows more secret things about you than you yourself are aware of.

Edgar Cayce could go into an autohypnotic coma in which you would tell him something about your dream. Your dreams contain the missing links in you. He could go into your dreams in his unconscious state and see the whole picture of it. Then he could tell you what your missing links are, because he could remember your whole dream.

You will be surprised that no one remembers his whole dream in the morning. It is impossible. The moment the conscious mind takes charge, it distorts the whole thing, because the message is from the unconscious. It is against the conscious, so the conscious mind distorts it, interprets it. It causes something to be missing, or something to be added, and then the whole thing becomes nonsense. You say, "This is just a dream—meaningless." No dream is meaningless. Dreams have a deeper meaning than your waking moments.

So a teacher has to work with your dreams. And unless he works with your dreams, he cannot work toward your awakening, because the dream-creating source inside you is the whole problem.

It has to be destroyed, it has to be uprooted from your consciousness. The complete mechanism of dreaming has to be broken, completely uprooted. When it is uprooted completely, first you will feel that you have lost dreaming and then you will feel that you have lost sleep. You will sleep, but something will remain aware. The body will be refreshed in the morning, but you will know that you have remained conscious.

If dreaming is lost, sleep will be lost. You may be surprised to learn that dreaming is a constant help to sleep. You cannot sleep without dreaming; dreaming helps you to continue your sleep. For example, if you feel hungry during sleep, your sleep will be broken. The body will break it. It will say, "Go and eat something." Or if you are feeling thirsty, your body will say, "Go and drink something." But the dream structure will help you to continue your sleep. It will create a dream. You are drinking water in the dream—then there is no need to break the sleep, then you can continue sleeping. You have taken something in the dream that was needed; the dream has substituted something for the real thing, and now you can continue sleeping.

Or, your alarm clock is ringing. It is five o'clock and you have to rise. The dream structure will create a dream: you are in a temple and a bell is ringing. The alarm clock ringing outside has been transferred and made part of the dream. Now the bell is ringing in the temple. There is no need to rise; you can continue sleeping.

So dreams help you to continue to sleep. Otherwise you cannot sleep. The sleep will be broken many times because there are so many happenings outside you. The body cannot tolerate them; even a single mosquito can disturb your sleep. But a dream can help there also. It may create a dream and the music of the mosquito will become the music of the dream. Then you dream and continue to sleep.

So the whole structure of the dreaming consciousness has to be uprooted. The teacher has to work to help this to happen. When he destroys the whole mechanism of dreaming, then and only then do the inner doors open and can he communicate directly.

Now there is no need of language, no need of words. He can communicate directly. And when there is a direct communication without words, only then can truth be revealed to you and not otherwise. So the most esoteric work is done with your dreaming consciousness—to change it.

Something of this secret may leak out. This has happened many times. There are whole sciences based on a single leak, a single indication that has come from the esoteric world. You can create a science, but it is always going to be faulty, imperfect. Freud's analysis of dreams can never be perfect because he does not know the whole science. Somewhere he stumbled across a single point and worked it out completely. But the point is just a part of the whole thing. The whole is not known.

When your dreaming consciousness has been washed away, then the real esoteric work begins. Then the teacher can take your hand in his hand and can lead you anywhere: to any reality, to any depths of the universe. But that cannot be talked about; it cannot be discussed. Teachers have led their pupils to heaven and hell, to every nook and corner of the universe—to every planet, to higher realms. But that only happens when your dreaming consciousness is gone completely. You cannot project anything; you have to become a screen. Then the world will be different for you because then you will be different. Really, the world will remain the same, but now you will not be projecting anything.

There are many more things that—if you are interested—you will have to go inside for. You cannot be informed about these things, but they can be made known to you, they can be known by you. I can help you, I can work with you, I can push you into an inner dimension, but I cannot inform you. Even everything that I am informing you of is more than is ever allowed. But I can inform you about many things that were never allowed because I always omit some key points.

Something is always missing from what I say—not to me, but to you. It is always missing until the phenomenon itself happens to you. Then everything will be complete; it will be linked. So I talk about many links, but there are always some missing links which will be discovered only by your own efforts. I talk about these unlinked links so that you may be persuaded to work hard. The more you work hard, the more missing links I will talk about. The chief link will never be talked about—it can only be experienced—but I am ready to help you to experience it. The nature of things is such that it can only be experienced.

Just do your part. And remember, you are capable of doing your part. Your part is to surrender; and whenever you are able to surrender, the teacher will come. The teacher is there, teachers have always been in existence. The world has never lacked teachers; it has always lacked disciples.

But no teacher can begin anything unless someone surrenders. So whenever you have a moment to surrender, do not lose it. If you do not find anyone to whom to surrender, then surrender to existence. But whenever there is a moment to surrender, do not lose it, because then you are on the border line: you are between sleep and waking. Just surrender!

If you can find someone to whom to surrender, that is good; but if you cannot find anyone, just surrender to the universe. And the teacher will appear; he will come. He rushes whenever there is surrender. When you become vacant, you become empty— spiritually you become empty—then the spiritual force rushes toward you and fills you.

So always remember that whenever you feel like surrendering, do not lose the moment. It may not come again or it may come only after centuries and lives have been unnecessarily wasted. Whenever the moment comes, just surrender.

But the mind has a trick. If you are angry, you will be angry that very moment. But if you feel like surrendering, you will think about it, you will plan about it, you will wait. And with the mind there is only one moment when it is on the boundary. So just surrender to the divine, to anything—even to a tree—because the real thing is not to whom you surrender; the real thing is the surrendering. Surrender to a tree and the tree will become a teacher to you. Many things will be revealed to you by the tree that no scripture can reveal to you. Surrender to a stone, and the stone will become a god and reveal things that no god can reveal to you.

The real thing is surrendering. Whenever there is surrendering, one always appears who becomes responsible for you. This is what is meant by initiation.

8

Esoteric Groups: Preservers and Mediators

Theosophists have talked about different groups of masters existing physically or even nonphysically. How many of these esoteric masters exist today? How do they influence sadhakas, seekers, and what is their affect on the world? Please tell us about your relationship with these esoteric groups of masters.

In order for spiritual knowledge to exist there are many difficulties. The first difficulty is that it cannot be expressed adequately. Even when someone comes to know it, he is not able to express it. So what has been known cannot be transferred easily.

Someone knows something and there are seekers who want to know it, but the knowledge cannot be communicated. Just because you want to know it, and just because someone else knows it and wants to tell it to you, doesn't mean that communication is possible. The very nature of spiritual knowledge is such that the moment you try to express it, you feel that it cannot be expressed. So to express it and communicate it esoteric groups are needed.

An esoteric group means a group specifically trained to receive a particular system of knowledge. For example, we may make an analogy. Einstein made reference many times to the fact that there existed not more than half a dozen people in the world with whom he could communicate. He was talking about mathematical knowledge, not about spiritual knowledge. But this was a fact. Not even half a dozen persons existed with whom Einstein could talk easily because he reached such peaks in mathematics that he could not communicate in ordinary mathematical symbols.

If Einstein tried to convey his knowledge to you, you would hear it, but not understand it. Just hearing is not understanding. And when you do not understand, there is every possibility that you will misunderstand because, from understanding to nonunderstanding, there is an in-between phenomenon of misunderstanding. No one is ready to accept that he has not understood, so when there is no understanding, it does not mean nonunderstanding. In ninety-nine cases out of a hundred, it means misunderstanding, because no one is ready to admit that he has not understood. Everyone will say that he understands, and then misunderstanding follows.

Mathematics is not an esoteric knowledge and is not concerned with the inexpressible. It has existed continuously for five thousand years. Thousands of minds are trained in mathematics. Every university all over the world teaches it; every primary school teaches it. With so much training, so much knowledge, so many departments in so many universities teaching it, Einstein still says, "Only six persons exist to whom I can communicate what I know." If you understand this, then you can begin to understand the difficulty of communicating spiritual experiences.

An esoteric group means a group that is specially trained to work with a particular teacher. A Buddha happens only after thousands of years. Because the phenomenon of Buddhahood is rare, when a Buddha happens, how will he be able to communicate? Buddha will be there, the world will be there, but it will not mean anything.

Buddha cannot communicate with the world directly, so an esoteric group, an inner group, is trained. The training is just so that this group can act as a mediator between Buddha and the world. A special group is specifically trained to understand Buddha and then to interpret Buddha to the world, because between a Buddha and the world there is such a gap that Buddha will not be understood at all.

To refer to Jesus here will be meaningful. Jesus suffered because there was no esoteric group. Jesus had to be crucified because the gap was such that the common people could not understand him. It had to happen, because there was not a group between Jesus and the common masses. There was no group which was able to understand Jesus and convey that understanding to the common masses. There was no mediator between the two, so Jesus suffered. In India, neither Buddha nor Mahavir suffered in this way. No one was crucified. They were as capable as Jesus, but only Jesus was crucified because no esoteric group existed for him. Misunderstanding was inevitable. Whatever Jesus said was misunderstood.

Of course, Jesus had a following, but the following was among the masses. All his chief disciples came from the masses without any esoteric training. Luke, Thomas—they were peasants; they were from the ordinary, uneducated part of society. They loved Jesus, they felt him, but they also could not understand him.

So there were many instances in which they asked very childish questions. For example, some disciples asked Jesus: "In the kingdom of God, what will be our position? You will be by the side of the divine, but where will we stand? What will be our position?" They could not understand what Jesus meant by the kingdom of God. They were common people.

But an esoteric group cannot be created suddenly. Buddha happens suddenly, but the group cannot be created suddenly. There is a Buddha—that is a sudden happening. So in countries that have been spiritual for thousands of years, esoteric groups exist as a continuity, as a tradition, and whenever there is this kind of happening, the group begins to work.

Ashoka created a group that is still existing—a group of nine persons. Whenever one person dies, another replaces him, so the group still continues. Whenever one person dies, the eight remaining ones will choose someone to replace him. He will be trained by the other eight and the group of nine continues. Persons change, but the group remains.

This group is still there today because a reincarnation of Buddha is awaited. He can come at any time. When Buddha is there you cannot suddenly create the group, because this group of esoteric adepts is created through long training and discipline. This training is not a happening; this group is a totally trained group. Everyone is trained; this is not a sudden happening. So the Ashoka group of nine is still existing.

Many times groups have been started. Sometimes they continue and then wither away. Sometimes they go on for a while and then are no more because there are so many difficulties. Many difficulties are there! But this esoteric group of Ashoka's still continues.

It continues because there are many conditions that help it to continue. One is that it never comes directly in contact with the masses itself. It has still other groups between. It always remains unknown, hidden. You can never know about it, its whereabouts. Any person who is initiated in the group—the very moment he is initiated, he disappears from your world, completely disappears. Then you can never know anything about him. Then the group can continue anonymously.

This group has many keys and many methods. Through those keys and methods, it goes on working in many ways. This is a group whose members are in the physical body. They are as alive as we are.

But once someone has become a member of the group, he cannot be chosen again to be part of the circle of nine in another life. In his next life, he will work as a link between the group and the masses. This creates another circle around the nine, a greater circle, because so many persons have been members of it. They know Buddha directly; they know the esoteric adepts directly. They are so experienced that they can remain in the masses and continue the work of the group, but they will not be its members.

When someone from the group is not born on earth, when he

is without a physical body—if he remains in a no-body existence
—he still continues to work. There are so many adepts who are
not in the physical body. They go on working. Theosophists call
them Masters—such as Master Koot Humi. These are fictitious
names but they refer to a particular personality, an individuality,
a particular unembodied soul that is still working.

Master Koot Humi, one of the most ancient adepts of Ashoka's
circle of nine, created the whole movement of theosophy. They
were trying to create a situation in which Buddha's coming incar-
nation could be possible. Buddha had said that after twenty-five
centuries he would again be born and his name would be Maitreya. An enlightened person like Gautama Buddha is capable of
knowing who is going to be enlightened twenty-five centuries
later. So Buddha predicted it, and for this happening, Ashoka's
circle of nine has been working for centuries.

Now the time is near. The theosophy movement was just a
preparation for the happening. It failed, the experiment failed.
They experimented with three or four people to be made vehicles
for Maitreya to descend, but the experiment failed. Something or
other missed. Sometimes the thing was just on the verge of success when something would happen to prevent it.

Krishnamurti was ready, completely ready to be made a vehicle.
Everything was ready. He came on the pulpit to surrender himself
and to become empty so that Maitreya could come in. But at the
last moment, he denied surrender. No one around him ever
thought that this could happen. Not even a hint was ever there
that Krishnamurti, in the final step, would fail and would come
back. That is why—after that phenomenon, after that happening
of coming back—for his whole life, continuously for forty years,
he has been emphasizing individuality: "Be an individual!"

This has a meaning. The whole preparation was to lose one's
individuality. Otherwise one cannot become a vehicle. "Be as if
you are not! Surrender totally to forces that are beyond you." But
just on the brink of jumping, he denied surrender. Everything was
ready. One step more and Maitreya would have entered the
world.

But the last step could not be taken. He came back. He said, "I am myself." That is why his whole philosophy became: do not surrender, do not follow, do not believe, do not be a disciple. The whole thing is just an outcome. It is just a rationalization and a consolation. For forty years continuously he has been working out of that final step, which was not taken. Still he is not out of it. The repentance is there, the wound is there. At the last moment, he could not surrender.

So theosophy failed with Krishnamurti and became a dead movement, because the movement existed for the materialization of this happening. It became meaningless. The house had been built, but the master never came to reside in it. So after Krishnamurti's refusal to be a vehicle for Maitreya, theosophy became meaningless. It still continues like a hangover, but nothing substantial exists in it now.

The whole movement was created by the nine adepts of Ashoka. They are still working. In many ways, they go on working. In fact, there is a history behind our so-called history that you cannot even conceive of. History has a deeper base. The periphery that we know as history is not the reality. Behind our so-called history continues another history, a deeper one about which we know nothing.

For example, take Hitler—his fascism, his whole movement, his desperate efforts to do something. No one knows that there was something hidden behind this. Hitler's movement was a movement that went wrong, an attempt that went counter to what its intention was. In the beginning, Hitler was just a vehicle for other forces. There are glimpses now that indicate he was not the real actor in the drama. He was just a means; he was just being used. Someone else was working behind him; other forces were using him. He was mad, he was a murderer—these were the manifestations of his own ego. Because he could not give up his ego, his prejudices, his madness, because he could not surrender his ego to the forces that were trying to work through him, the attempt failed. It went against its own intentions.

Look at Hitler's choice of the swastika. The swastika, the symbol of Adolf Hitler's party, is the oldest, the most ancient symbol of a particular school of adepts. One of the most ancient groups in India is the Jains. The swastika is their symbol. But it is not exactly the same as the symbol Hitler used. Hitler's swastika design was in reverse order: the Jains' swastika is clockwise; Hitler's is anticlockwise.

This anticlockwise swastika is a destructive symbol. The clockwise swastika is a great creative symbol. The Nazis searched three years for a symbol, because a symbol is not just a symbol. If you take a symbol from a deeper tradition, then the symbol becomes a link. So persons were sent by Hitler to Tibet in order to discover one of the most ancient symbols of the Aryan race. With that symbol, it was known that much which is hidden could be contacted. So the swastika was chosen, but in reverse order.

The person who discovered the symbol, Hessenhoff, convinced Adolf Hitler that the symbol should be in reverse order. He was one of the persons who was in contact with many esoteric groups. But he was confused. He was searching for two things: first, for a symbol that was very ancient, and second, for a symbol that could also be made new. Because of this, the swastika was chosen and made in reverse order. It had never existed that way before.

But due to this, events took on an altogether different shape. Because of the reversal of the symbol, all over the world those who were in contact with any esoteric knowledge knew that Hitler was going to destroy himself. He would become mad; he would be in contact with suicidal forces.

The entire concept behind Hitler's philosophy was given by hidden schools. They used him just as Krishnamurti was going to be used by the theosophists and the hidden groups. That is why Hitler continued winning up to a certain point, up to a certain moment. He was only winning; there was no defeat. The thing was phenomenal. He could win anything; it looked as if he were undefeatable. But after a certain time, everything began to go the other way. Why did this happen?

Forces against nazism defeated Hitler, but that is not the real history. That is just an outward phenomenon. Hitler was used by an esoteric group. This was one of the most desperate efforts made by the group. For centuries this esoteric group was working, but they could not help humanity as they desired to. This was a last, desperate effort to help humanity before humanity destroyed itself on earth. They had tried before through saints, through persons who were powerless, who were poor in spirit. Now, through Adolf Hitler, they tried to win the whole world before it was destroyed, and to give a certain teaching to humanity. But just as Krishnamurti became independent at the last moment, Hitler also became independent. That is why he was finally defeated.

What happened with Hitler was a miracle in war history. It has never happened before like this. Hitler would not take the advice of any general. He would move or attack, but no advice of any general would be taken. Even against the advice of all his trained people, he would act and move as he liked. And still he would win. There were absurd moves, nonsensical moves. No one who knew anything about war would have taken those moves. But Hitler would take them and win. Everyone around him knew that he was just a vehicle of some greater force. Otherwise, what happened was not explainable.

And whenever he gave an order, he would not be in his conscious mind. This is a fact that has just become known now. Whenever he would give an order, he would be ecstatic. His eyes would be closed. He would begin to tremble, he would perspire, and then his voice would change completely; another voice would give the order. But the day he began to fall, his own voice began to give the orders. From that point on, from that moment on, he was never in ecstasy. Some contact that had been working was lost.

Now, those who study Hitler and his life all feel that the phenomenon was not merely political. The person himself was not just a political maniac, not just a mad politician, because whatever he did was absolutely nonpolitical—his whole approach. Those who remained with him felt that he was a split personality. In his ordinary moments he was so ordinary that you could not conceive of it. There was no magic; he was just ordinary. But when he was taken over, possessed, he was an altogether different personality.

Who was behind this? Some esoteric group was behind it, and that esoteric group was trying to do something. When Hitler became independent he lost every power: in his last days he was just ordinary. And after this particular moment, when he lost contact, whatever he did went against him. Before this, whatever he did was always in his favor.

The same group about whom I have been talking to you—the Ashoka nine—was behind the whole thing. They were trying to capture the whole world. With man it is possible that if you begin to work with some force behind you, you yourself may not be aware of it. If you succeed, then you are not aware that someone else is succeeding. *You* succeed; your ego is strengthened. And there comes a moment when your ego is so strengthened that you will not listen to any force. This has happened many times.

The esoteric group, as I said to you before, functions primarily as a continuity, so that whenever there is any need, an esoteric group will be there to help. And they can help in many ways.

It was not just a coincidence that Japan became friendly to Germany. It was because of this group of nine people. This is the hidden fact. The esoteric group that was working behind Hitler was a Buddhist group, so a Buddhist country, Japan, could be influenced to side with Hitler. The whole East felt exhilarated when Hitler was winning. The whole East was inwardly with Hitler because the group that was working behind him was an Eastern group. Nothing happens accidentally. Everything has a causal link behind it.

Whenever a teacher like Buddha happens, the primary work of an esoteric group is to help by becoming a mediator. Another work of these esoteric groups is to preserve the knowledge once it is obtained. Buddha attained something supreme, but who will preserve it? Preserving something in books is no preservation because the knowledge is so alive and books are so dead. Only words can be preserved in books, not knowledge. Knowledge can be preserved only by living persons, not by books, because books will have to be interpreted again—and who will interpret them? They will have to be decoded again—and who will decode them? If someone is able to decode them, to interpret them rightly, then that person can give you the message without the books. But those who depend on the books will not be able to interpret them rightly.

You cannot read any book that you have not known already in some way. You can only read yourself and nothing else. If you are reading Buddha's *Dhammapada,* it is not Buddha's *Dhammapada* you are reading; it is your *Dhammapada.* Now you will be the creator of it. Now your depths will reach to the depths of Buddha's sayings. You cannot go beyond yourself; you cannot have a glimpse of anything that is beyond yourself.

So whenever knowledge is attained—subtle knowledge, foundational knowledge, ultimate knowledge—it cannot be preserved in books. Only ordinary knowledge, which cannot be misinterpreted, which any ordinary school can train you to interpret, can be preserved in books. If you know the language, you can know it. But supreme knowledge cannot be preserved that way. It can be preserved only through living persons. Hence the esoteric group. Then the knowledge is transferred from one living person to another. And the transfer is not a mechanical transfer; it is an art.

I will tell you a story, a very esoteric one. There is a Buddhist story of a master thief. He was so efficient, such a master, that he could not be caught. Whenever he broke into a house he would leave behind something to show that the master thief had entered. His art became so famous that if he came to one house and not another, the others would be jealous—because the master thief went to the houses only of those who were worthy of his skills. Even the emperor of the country wanted to meet him!

Everything the thief was going to do would be declared ahead of time. When he was going to rob someone, first there would be a rumor about it. The person would be notified somehow that the master thief was coming soon. "Make any arrangements you want to make. On such-and-such a day, at such-and-such a time, there will be a robbery." And the thief was never caught.

Then he became old and his son asked him, "Now you are old and I do not know even the ABCs of your art. Let me be trained."

The father said, "It is difficult. It is not a science; it is not a question of technical know-how. I cannot teach you unless you are a born thief. Then only is it possible. It is so artistic; it is a creative art. I have lived it. It has not been an evil to me; it has been my spirit. So we will see."

One night he asked his son to follow him. They went to a palace. He broke through the wall. His age was sixty-five or seventy, but there was no trembling in his hands. And the son was young and strong but he was perspiring even though the night was cold. He was trembling. His father said, "Why are you trembling? Just be a witness. Why are you trembling?" But the more he tried not to tremble, the more he trembled. And his father went on working as if he were in his own house.

They went inside. The father unlocked a door and asked his son to go in. He went in, and the father locked the door behind him. Then the father made such noises that the whole house was awakened. He ran away, leaving his son locked inside the closet. The whole household began searching for the thief. You can imagine what was happening inside the boy!

The father went to his house. The night was cold. He went to his bed and relaxed. After two hours the son came running in. He pulled at his father's blanket and said, "You nearly killed me! Is this the way to train me?"

The father looked at him and said, "Oh, are you back? Good! Do not tell me the story of what happened. It is irrelevant. Do not go into details. You are back? That is good. The art has been transferred."

The son was uneasy about talking but still he said, "Let me tell you first that you nearly killed me! How cruel you are to your only son!"

The father said, "Tell me what happened, not what you did. What happened after I locked the door?"

The son said, "I became another person. Death was so near!

I never before felt such energy as that which came to me. Everything was at stake—life or death. I became so acutely aware. I have never been so aware before. I became awareness itself because each moment was precious. One way or the other, everything was to be decided. Then some maid passed by the door with a candle in her hand. You asked rightly, 'What happened?' because I cannot say 'I' did it. But somehow I made a noise as if a cat were inside. She unlocked the door, opened it, and looked inside with her candle.

"I cannot say I did anything. I just blew out the candle, pushed her and ran. I began to run with such a force that I cannot say 'I' was running. The running happened. 'I' was not; I was completely not. There was just a force moving.

"They followed me. I passed a deep well. It happened. I cannot say 'I' did it, but I took a stone and threw it in the well. They all surrounded the well and they thought that the thief had fallen in. So now I am here."

But the father was fast asleep. He had not even heard the story. In the morning he said, "Details are irrelevant. Art cannot be told, only shown through living examples, through constant communion."

Supreme knowledge can be transferred and preserved. Sometimes these esoteric groups have preserved knowledge for centuries for a particular person who was being awaited so that this knowledge could be transferred to him.

For example, Mahavir had fifty thousand monks. All could not be enlightened in his lifetime, so many remained somewhere on the path. Mahavir was not going to be in the world again, but those who were somewhere on this path must be supplied with further knowledge. Who will supply it? Mahavir will not be here and scriptures cannot be relied on because they are absurd. Someone will have to interpret them, but they cannot be interpreted beyond the understanding of the one who is interpreting, so it is meaningless. There must be a group which preserves keys that can be handed to persons in a particular state of mind. Otherwise these people will be lost or they will have to struggle unnecessarily, meaninglessly.

Or, they will have to change teachers. But whenever someone changes teachers he has to begin anew, because nothing of the old system can be used in the new. Nothing from this path can be used on that path; every path has its own organic unity. What is meaningful on Mohammed's path is not meaningful on Mahavir's path. What is meaningful on Buddha's path is not meaningful on Jesus' path. So if someone comes from the Buddhist path to Jesus' path, he will have to begin anew. All the efforts of past lives will be thrown. That is not good; that is a sheer waste.

So when the teacher is not there, these esoteric groups preserve knowledge and that knowledge then begins to work as a teacher. But the knowledge can only be preserved by living persons. Of these nine persons in Ashoka's circle, each one is an adept in a particular key. Individually they do not have all the keys; each one is a specialist in a particular key.

The group was formed with nine people because Buddha talked about nine doors, nine keys, nine kinds of knowledge. Each person is adept in only one key; he knows about only one door. Those who want to enter from that door can be helped by him. Buddha can know about nine doors, but these nine people cannot know about nine doors. Only one door is enough; to know one key of one door is enough. You need not enter from nine doors. One door will do—you will be inside.

So these nine adepts each have one key. Each one of them knows everything about one door, one meditative path. Whenever a need is there, the right one will help. The help may be direct, the help may be indirect, but he will help.

Whenever a new Buddha is coming, or a new enlightened one is coming, the group will prepare the ground. They will prepare people to listen to him, to understand him. If there were no such ground prepared, then every teacher would be crucified—crucified because there would be no group to help make the people understand him.

There are other esoteric groups that work in other ways. Sometimes it happens that humanity forgets what it had previously known. Somewhere *The Book of the Dead*—the Egyptian book —says, "Ignorance is nothing but forgetfulness." Something that was known has been forgotten. In a way, nothing is new. Something has just been forgotten and when you come to know it again, it appears to be new.

Many times many keys are lost, sometimes because there are no esoteric groups to preserve them. Sometimes the group is there, but nobody is ready to be initiated in the knowledge. Then the esoteric group cannot do anything other than preserve. And sometimes even preservation becomes impossible. It is not so easy. If one person dies out of a group of nine, it is not always easy to replace him, because the replacement is not through any election. It is not democratic. Knowledge cannot depend on democracy; only ignorance can.

Knowledge is always autocratic, always. You cannot decide by election who will be head of the atomic commission. And if you decide that, your decision will be its own suicide. Knowledge is always autocratic. It is never from below; it is always from above.

Try to see this distinction clearly. Anything that comes from below is bound to come from ignorance. Politics is ignorance par excellence. It comes from below. The one who is the lowest chooses the one who is highest. And what is meant by the highest? The lowest decides the highest, so the highest must be lower than the lowest. In a democracy, leaders are nothing but followers of their followers. Knowledge cannot depend on this. Knowledge is always given from above and therefore is autocratic.

Esoteric groups maintain keys, preserve knowledge. The moment someone becomes capable of being given a particular system of knowledge, a particular secret, then that key is delivered. Until someone is ready, the group waits. It may have to wait for centuries.

It is very difficult to replace one person from the group who has died. The replacement cannot be decided by choice. The eight remaining members of the group have to find a person who is capable, and even a capable person has to be trained before he can enter the group. Sometimes the group works on a person for many lives and only then does the person become capable of replacing a member. And if no one is found, the key is lost and cannot be found again by this esoteric group. It can be found again only when a person like Buddha happens. The esoteric group can only preserve, communicate. It cannot discover; discovery is not within their capacity. So, many keys are lost.

Many groups have worked, and many are still working. The Rosicrucians have been a parallel group in the West. It has worked for centuries. Really, it is not a Christian group; it is more ancient than the Christians. Rosicrucians are part of the esoteric group of the Rosy Cross. The cross is not really a Christian symbol; it is older than Christ. Christ himself was initiated by an esoteric group known as the Essenes. So all Christian holy days —for example, Easter or Christmas—are older than Christ. Christianity only absorbed the old tradition.

Jesus himself belonged to an esoteric group that conveyed many things to him which he then tried to convey to the masses. This group tried to prepare the ground for Jesus but it could not be made ready, it could not function well. We all know that John the Baptist came before Jesus and that for thirty to forty years he continued with just one teaching: "I am only the forerunner. The real one is still to come. I have come just to prepare the ground and when the real one comes, I will disappear."

He remained on the banks of the Jordan River for forty years, baptizing people. He was baptizing everyone, initiating everyone, for the sake of the "real one" who was to follow. Everyone kept asking, "Who is to come?" The whole country was excited about the one who was to come. His name was not known even to John the Baptist. He, also, had to wait.

John the Baptist belonged to the Essenes. Christ had been one of the important initiated members of the Essene group in his past life.

Finally, Jesus came to be baptized by John the Baptist. And the day Jesus was baptized, John the Baptist disappeared forever. He baptized Jesus in the Jordan River and shortly afterward was never seen again. When this happened, the news spread that the real one had come. For forty years continuously, John the Baptist had been telling people that when the real one comes, "I will baptize him as the last one, and then I will disappear." And John the Baptist disappeared. So baptism is pre-Christian, before Christ. Baptism was there and then Christianity began. This John the Baptist belonged to a particular esoteric group: the Essenes.

There are many groups, but the difficulty always comes when someone dies and there is no one who can replace him. Then there is a missing link. In every teaching, that missing link appears. And when a missing link appears, you cannot be helped by the group because the gaps cannot be filled. There are gaps in Christianity now, many gaps. There are gaps in every teaching. If one part is lost, it cannot be replaced unless a person like Jesus happens again. But that is not predictable; that cannot be arranged; that cannot be planned. Only a group of initiated seekers can be planned and created. Then they can be used whenever there is someone who is capable of using them.

These esoteric groups are not concerned with this earth alone. Now even scientists agree that at least fifty thousand planets other than earth must have life. More is possible, but less is not possible. In such a great universe, by the ordinary laws of probability, at least fifty thousand planets must have life. So the esoteric group has another task to do: to link the knowledge of one planet to another. That is a little more difficult because we have not known everything. We may be missing something that was known previously, we may be knowing something only partially. On another planet there may now be a greater knowledge than ours; on another planet there may now be another Buddha.

The esoteric group works as an inner link between different systems of knowledge that exist anywhere in the universe, so missing links can be supplied from other planets also. And, really, it always happens so. Whenever something is missing and we cannot call upon a person on this earth to appear and discover it, then the knowledge can be supplied from another planet. It always exists somewhere else.

The esoteric group can be in contact with everything that exists in the whole universe. This work is as valuable as someone from a university going to a primitive village. The primitive village does not know anything; the university man knows. This man can train the primitive man to receive the knowledge. Then he can deliver it and still be in contact with his source of knowledge.

This is just an analogy. But many times this planet has been visited by other planetary beings. They have left many landmarks. Sometimes they have left many keys of knowledge on this planet with some group. Then those groups have been working. So esoteric groups are interplanetary.

Each age has to devise its own methods. No old methods can be really helpful to you. You have changed: your mind has changed. The key is exactly the same as it was in the past, but the lock has changed. Esoteric groups can only be the preservers of keys not of locks, because the locks are within you. Do you understand it?

Locks are with you—not with Buddha, not with Jesus. They have keys. They devise keys, keys that open many locks. These keys can be preserved by esoteric groups, but in the meantime the locks are changing. You are not the same lock that Buddha opened. The same key, exactly as it is, will not do. If the same key can do, as it is, then any ignorant person can use it. Then no wisdom is needed, anybody can use it. I can give you the key and you can go and open the lock; you need no wisdom. This much is enough: this is the key and that is the lock. But because the locks are changing constantly, the keys must be given to a group that is wise enough to devise new keys out of these old keys, so that the keys are always in tune with the locks.

The locks will go on changing, they will never be the same. So not only are dead keys to be preserved, but also the science for

changing the keys whenever there is any change in the lock must
be known. That knowledge is preserved by esoteric groups. You
cannot preserve it in books because the locks are not known: they
will change, they will go on changing. No book can write about
all the possibilities of locks, about all the combinations of locks.
They will go on changing. The condition changes, education
changes, culture changes, everything changes, so the locks become different. However the key is preserved, it will always be
faulty in a way, it will not suit the lock. So the key must be handed
over to a living group of wise ones who are able to change the key
also.

That is the difference between esoteric knowledge and exoteric
tradition. Exoteric tradition always carries the key without any
reference to the lock. It continues to talk about the old key. It
never notices that no lock is being opened by it. But the tradition
consists of ordinary people—that is, people like the members of
the Christian Church. The Church carries the key: they know
that this key opened many doors in Jesus' time. Their knowledge
is right; their information is correct. Of course, this key has
opened many locks! So they carry the key, they worship the key.
But now the key opens no lock. And they cannot devise other
keys; they have no time to devise keys. They only have one key,
so they go on worshiping it, and if it cannot open a lock, then the
lock itself is responsible. Then the lock must be faulty; then
something is wrong with the lock, not with the key.

The exoteric tradition is always condemning the lock and worshiping the key. An esoteric group never condemns the lock; it
always changes the key. The Vatican carries the key—they have
the key, they go on worshiping it—but Christianity also has inner
esoteric groups. And this always happens: the esoteric group will
be in conflict with the exoteric, because the exoteric tradition
will always insist that only its key will do. The key does not exist
for you; you exist for the key. You must behave in such a way that
this key can open the lock. The key cannot be changed; you must
change. And if someone says, "We can change the key," he

becomes known as an infidel, he becomes known as a heretic. Then he must be killed because of the nonsense he is speaking. He changed the key: the key that Jesus gave us, or Buddha gave us, or Mahavir gave us. This key *cannot* be changed.

So always, whenever there is a teacher, an authentic teacher who discovers something, there are two currents that come from him. One current becomes the exoteric tradition, the visible Church: with the Pope, or with Shankaracharya—the orthodox. They always insist on the same key; they never think that a key means nothing if it cannot open any lock.

But then it is not a key at all. A key only means that which opens some lock. If it does not open any lock, then it is fallacious to call it a key. It is just a linguistic fallacy. It is not a key at all. It becomes a key only when a lock opens with it. When you are putting something in your pocket it is not a key; it is only a possible key. When it opens the lock, it becomes the actual key. If it does not open any lock, it even loses the possibility of being a key. But the visible Church is always obsessed with the key because the key has been given by an authentic teacher.

Every authentic teacher also creates an inner circle. That inner circle has the key *and* the knowledge of how to change it in certain circumstances. This inner circle will always be in conflict with the outer because the outer will think that the inner is inferior and is changing the key the master gave. "Who are you to do that? How can you change the key?"

For example, in Islam some Sufis had esoteric knowledge but Mohammedans killed them. Mansoor was killed because he was talking about many changes in the key. The esoteric group is always interested in the lock, not obsessed with the key. The exoteric group is obsessed with the key, but is not interested in the lock at all. If it opens, it is good. If it does not open, you are responsible—the key is never responsible.

The Mohammedans have many Sufi orders—inner circles. They are inner groups. Mohammedans thought that these inner groups were working in a very rebellious way, so many Sufis were killed. Ultimately, they had to disappear. So now there are many

Sufis, but you cannot know them. Someone may be just a sweeper. You will never even be able to detect that this man may be a Sufi. Unless someone introduces you to the fact, you will never be aware of it. He may be coming to your house daily and still you will never be aware that this is someone who has some key.

Or he may be just a shoemaker. He will continue with his shoemaking and you may think that those who are sitting with him are just being trained in the art of shoemaking. There *are* some customers, but there may also be some disciples working with the shoemaker who are not just being trained in shoemaking. This shoemaking business is just a façade. Inside, something else is going on.

So Sufis had to disappear completely because the outer tradition would not tolerate them. They would just be killed, because if these inner ones continue, then there is no future for the outward tradition. It becomes absolutely meaningless.

Only he is a teacher who has discovered himself, who has devised a key himself, who has known the source of knowledge himself, who has encountered the reality himself. And after him, there are two schools.

Certain teachers never allowed any exoteric groups. In Buddha's time there were seven other teachers of the same rank as Buddha. You may not even have heard their names. Only one name is known—Mahavir. Another six are completely unknown. They also had keys—knowledge—as much as Buddha and Mahavir, but they never allowed any exoteric group to be formed around them. Only the inner circle continued in some way, somewhere. There was one man, Prabuddha Katyayan, another was Purna Kashyas, another Ajit Keshkambal, who were of the same level, of the same rank, of the same inner realization as Buddha and Mahavir. But no one even knows their names. Their names are only known at all because Buddha mentioned them somewhere. No scripture about them can be found, no following, no temple, no church. But they still continue in a very hidden and subtle way, and no one can say they have not helped many. They have helped. They are not known to many, but they have helped as many as any Buddha.

Buddha's name is known; the whole world knows about him. But the more we know about him, the less we can use him. He also has inner circles working for him. Only these are meaningful. But they always come in conflict with the outer religious order. And the outer order is a powerful force because the masses are with it.

Buddha created a chosen circle. He created his circle with a person by the name of Mahakashyap. This name is mentioned only once. Sariputra and Modgalayan—these were his chief disciples of the exoteric order. Their names are known all over the world; they have shrines in their honor. But the real, authentic key was given to Mahakashyap—not to Sariputra, not to Modgalayan. Still, his name is mentioned only once—only once in the whole Buddhist scripture. I will narrate the incident to you again.

Buddha came one day with a flower in his hand. He was going to give a sermon. But no sermon was given—he just sat silently, looking at the flower. Everyone wondered what he was doing. Then everyone became uneasy. It continued for ten minutes, twenty minutes, thirty minutes. Then everyone became more uneasy; no one was able to say what he was doing. They all had gathered, at least ten thousand people, to hear him speak, and he was just sitting, only looking at the flower. In this incident, the name of Mahakashyap is mentioned.

Someone laughed. Buddha looked up and said, "Mahakashyap, come to me." The person who laughed was Mahakashyap. Only this one time has he been mentioned in the scriptures. Buddha gave the flower to Mahakashyap and said, "All that could be said I have said to all, and all that could not be said I have given to Mahakashyap." This is the only incident; that's all. Never before and never after is anything about Mahakashyap known—neither who he was nor where he was born.

Why is the whole Buddhist scripture so silent about him? Such an important person to whom Buddha says, "I give to Mahakashyap all that cannot be said"! Of course, the essential thing is what cannot be said. Only the nonessential can be said, only the superficial can be said, only the utilitarian can be said. The most significant transfer of knowledge is possible in silence only.

But never again is Mahakashyap's name mentioned. For centuries, no one knows what happened to Mahakashyap. Then, after eleven hundred years, a person in China declared, "I am in direct contact, in the direct chain, of Mahakashyap." After eleven hundred years someone declared in China, "I belong to Mahakashyap. I am his disciple." He was Bodhidharma.

No Indian scripture mentions Bodhidharma. He was born in India, lived three-fourths of his life in India, but no one knows anything about him. Where was he? What was he doing? Suddenly, he appears in China and says, "I belong to Mahakashyap, the man to whom Buddha gave the flower. I have the flower with me, still fresh." Of course! He is talking about something that can never be other than fresh.

Someone asks, "Where is the flower?"

Bodhidharma says, "It is standing before you. *I* am that flower! Buddha transferred this flower to Mahakashyap and now I have come to seek the right person to transfer the flower to, because I am going to die now. This is my last birth. I have traveled from India to China with certain information: someone is here to whom the flower can be delivered. I have come seeking him. But the same source of information has informed me that I must not go to him—he must come to me—so I will just wait."

What does he mean by this "source of information"? Esoteric groups go on informing the persons who need to be informed.

Bodhidharma said, "But the same source has informed me that I must not seek him," because sometimes a direct seeking becomes an interference. If I have come to your house it will be quite different from your coming to me. It is not the same. If I have come to your house you will be closed to me, but if you come to me, you will be open. *You* have come.

Bodhidharma said, "The same source of information has said to me that I must wait. And the same source has also given me a particular indication of how I should know who the person is to whom the flower is to be transferred."

He sat for nine years without facing anyone, just facing the wall. Many people came to him. Even the emperor of China, Wu, came to meet him, but Bodhidharma did not turn his face. He just sat facing the wall. Wu's courtier told him that the emperor was coming and tried to persuade him that it was very unmannerly to sit before the emperor facing the wall. Bodhidharma said, "I am not going to the emperor; the emperor is coming to me. He can choose to come to the unmannerly Bodhidharma or not; he is free. I am not coming to him."

When Emperor Wu heard what Bodhidharma had said, he came to him. He had to come; it became an obsession. He had no other way of checking to see if the man was worth visiting.

He came. Bodhidharma was sitting facing the wall. Wu asked him, "Why are you facing the wall? Why will you not look at me? Why will you not look at others?"

Bodhidharma said, "For my whole life I was facing you and all the others, but in your eyes I never saw anything other than a dead wall. So I decided that it is better to face the wall. One is at ease if one knows that there is a wall, but if you are facing someone and you feel that a wall is there, it becomes difficult. I can talk to you more easily because you are behind me and I am not seeing you."

For nine years continuously he sat facing the wall like this. Finally, the person came for whom he had certain information.

This person, Hui-Neng, came. He cut off his hand, gave it to Bodhidharma, and said, "Make a complete turnabout, otherwise I will cut off my head!"

Bodhidharma took a complete turn, faced Hui-Neng, and said, "I deliver to you the flower. I was waiting. A certain source of knowledge had given me the sign that the person would come, would cut off his hand and put it before me, and if I delayed a second he would cut off his head. Do not be in such a hurry. I am ready to give you the things for which I have traveled from India to China."

That secret cult has now flowered into the exoteric cult of Zen. Zen Buddhism is just an exoteric cult around this esoteric Bodhidharma tradition. Now, whatever Suzuki or others around the world are talking about is from the exoteric knowledge, not from the esoteric one. Now the esoteric root has become hidden again; it has again disappeared. But the current is there; it continues. So that is why there are esoteric circles. For so many reasons they exist.

You ask me if I am connected with any esoteric groups. If you can be in contact with one, you can be in contact with all. It is just a matter of tuning. If your radio can work with one station, there is no difficulty in its working with another. If the mechanism is working rightly, you can catch any station around the world. If you can be in contact with one esoteric group, you can be in contact with all. You may not want to be in contact, or you may want to be, but once you know the tuning—once you know how you can be in contact—you can be in contact.

Whatever I am saying is, in many ways, esoteric. That is why many times I become very confusing to you. No exoteric teaching is ever confusing. It is clear-cut; it is just like "two plus two equals four." It is always a simple thing. But the esoteric—the inner, the secret—is difficult to understand because your ability to understand becomes disturbed when any knowledge that is totally new to you has to be absorbed. Any knowledge that you know the basic principles of, you can absorb easily. It can become a part of you; you can digest it. But anything that is totally new to you has to be digested. No esoteric knowledge can be delivered in mathematical terms. It has to be delivered mystically, it has to be delivered poetically. It means many things simultaneously. Then it becomes alive.

I have been in contact with many esoteric groups. I have known many living persons who belong to some esoteric group. I have known many keys that were delivered by authentic teachers. But no key from an old tradition is enough, so I am devising new keys. And because I am devising new keys, I am not directly concerned with any esoteric group. Each esoteric group is interested in, and entrusted with, a particular key to preserve. I am not interested in a particular key. I am interested in devising new methods, new techniques, new keys, because all the old keys have become irrelevant in many ways.

One thing has to be understood: all these keys were developed in a world that was local—always local. For the first time, we are in a world that is absolutely nonlocal—universal. Really, for the first time we are in a *world*. Before, we were always confined to a particular *part* of the world. So the earlier keys were developed for particular local conditions and cultures.

Now, in a way, the world is in a mess for the first time. There is no particular culture, there is no particular conditioning. Everything is mixed up. And this is going to be more and more the case. Soon there will be a world citizenry with no local background at all, with a universal background. So before this century ends we will need—we are already in need of—keys that are universal.

For example, Jesus' key was for the use of a particular Jewish group. This is really an irony of history: Jesus invented a key, devised a key, for the Jewish mind, and now the Jews are against him and those who follow him are against the Jews. But the key was particularly devised for a Jewish-conditioned mind. As far as I am concerned, Christ's key can be used more easily by a Jew than by a Christian because the Christian is a product of a later development. Jesus never knew any Christian. He himself was not a Christian, but a Jew. But this is the irony of our history.

Buddha devised a key for a particular mind. Now that particular mind exists only in India, but his key is nowhere to be found in India. It exists in China, Japan, Ceylon, Burma, and Tibet, but not in India. And he devised a key particularly for Hindu minds! He was born a Hindu and he died a Hindu—he never knew anything about Buddhism. So the key was developed for the Hindu mind and then, around the key, there developed a sect that is opposed to Hinduism. Then the key becomes irrelevant. It is not of any use for anyone except for a particular Hindu mind. But this is the irony of history. It always happens so.

So I am struggling to devise keys that are, in a way, universal —not for a particular localized culture, but for the human mind as such. Soon we will be needing universal keys; these local keys will not do. Nor will any amalgamation do—just to put all the old keys together. That creates even more nonsense. You are unlocking one lock with many keys: something from the Koran, some thing from the Bible, something from Buddha, something from Mahavir.

There are many people with very good wishes doing much wrong. They talk about the unity of all religions. That is like talking about using all the keys there are to open one lock— unifying all the keys. One is enough! Too many keys will not enable you to open a lock. Any one key *might* have opened it, but too many keys will only create confusion.

These traditional keys are all local keys. They developed in a world that was divided. There was no universal mind; there never has been as far as our so-called knowledge of history is concerned. Sometimes the phenomenon of a universal mind has happened, but that is beyond the history of our civilization, beyond our memory.

Sometimes in the past, this phenomenon has also happened— that there was a universal mind. But it has been completely forgotten. For example, I will tell you one or two things.

In England, they change the date at midnight. That makes no sense really; it looks absurd. No one will awaken out of his sleep just to change the date. It is illogical, impractical. The date must be changed in the morning, that is common sense. So why does the date change in the night in England? Why has this become the rule? There is a reason for it. It is because when it is 5:30 in the morning in India, it is midnight in England.

There was a time, before this civilization, when the Hindu mind ruled the whole world. When the British Empire was spread all over the world, Greenwich Time was the mean time, the real time. Everyone would refer to it. In the same way, before the Mahabharati War, when the Hindu mind ruled the world, when it was morning in India that was the time to change the date. It was midnight then in England, so they changed the calendar date then. With the fall of the British Empire, Greenwich Time has been forgotten and someday no one will know about it, but the calendar date has continued to change according to Indian time.

You will be surprised that the English Parliament made a special act three hundred years ago to begin the calendar year on

January 1. Before three hundred years ago, the calendar date in England ended with March 25. How can the year end with March 25? There is no meaning to it. But that was the day in which the Indian year ends and this was copied all over the world. So Parliament had to make a special act to change it.

The word "december" means the tenth month, but December is the twelve month. Why was this name chosen for the tenth month? December means *dush* (ten) in Sanskrit and this is the tenth month in the Indian year. Somehow, the old tradition continued. The last week of the month of December is known all over the world as Xmas. *X* is the Roman numeral for ten and *mas* means month in Sanskrit. Xmas means the tenth month. But why is this in December? December should not be the tenth. It is so because this is the tenth month in the Indian calendar. But this whole tradition goes back to before the Mahabharati War happened, about five thousand years ago.

In the *Mahabharat,* there are stories about Arjuna being married to a Mexican girl. The Sanskrit word *maxika* became Mexico. The Mexican civilization that existed then had so many Hindu symbols that you cannot help but say that it was a Hindu civilization. The whole Mexican civilization was Hindu: Hindu temples, Hindu gods—even the deity Ganesh was found there. But now it is almost as if that never was.

We have come again only recently to a universal world in which Arjuna can marry a Mexican girl. Soon there will be no localized culture. And for this unfocused culture we have to devise new, broader, more fluid keys, less solid and more fluid—keys that can be used with many locks.

I have known so many esoteric groups. In this life and before, I have been in contact with many esoteric groups. But I cannot tell you their whereabouts, I cannot tell you their names, because that is not permitted. And that is of no use, really. But I can tell you that they still exist, they still try to help.

Some groups are still very much alive, for example, Ashoka's group. If Ashoka has done something more meaningful than any other emperor anywhere in the world, it is the creation of this esoteric group of nine men. Akbar tried to imitate Ashoka in many ways. He also created a group of nine, but it was meaningless. They were just courtiers—*Nava Ratna,* the nine jewels of Akbar. But they were just imitation jewels—exoteric. One person was a poet, someone else a warrior. That makes no sense. Akbar knew from somewhere that Ashoka had a group of nine—nine wise men—so he created a group of nine jewels. But he didn't know anything about Ashoka's group, so what he did was meaningless.

The Ashoka group has persisted for two thousand years. It is still alive, with the key—still working. The whole theosophical movement was initiated by this group. That is why Buddha became the most significant figure in theosophy. All of theosophy in a way has been Buddhist or Hindu, which is why, in Western countries, it was thought to be an Eastern effort to convert the West—that it was just Hinduism working in a new garb. In a sense it is true that it is Eastern, because the initiator group was a Buddhist group.

You can also be in contact with esoteric groups. There are techniques and methods to do it. But you will have to do much work on yourself. As you are, you can never be in contact. You will just pass by an esoteric circle, but you will not even be able to detect it. You will have to change yourself, tune yourself to a new dimension. For new vibrations to be felt, you will have to become more sensitive. Then you will not ask me if I have been in contact with any esoteric groups. You will know just by sitting near me; you will know just by looking into my eyes. You will feel it. Just by hearing my words, or even by hearing my silence, you will understand.

But that will come only if you change yourself, attune yourself to a new reality, if you open yourself up to new dimensions. Esoteric groups are, and always have been, there. Only you are closed: closed in thought, closed in thinking, closed within yourself—no opening, no window, no door. The sky is there: just open the window and you will know the sky and the stars.

However far off they may be, just by opening your window, which is so near, you come in contact with far-off stars. In a way it is illogical. By opening such a nearby thing, how can you come in contact with far-off stars? If I tell you, "Open the window behind you, and you will come in contact with the whole universe," you will say, "It is absurd. Just by opening this window, which is so near, how can I be in contact with what is so far away?"

But it is so. Open a window in your mind, create a window of meditation, and you will be in contact with many far-off lights, with many happenings that are always around. Just around the corner, right near you, everything is happening, but you are blind or asleep—or just unaware.

I am *here*, but you cannot conceive of what is happening here. You cannot conceive of it!

I was a student at the university. The vice-chancellor spoke on the day of Buddha's birthday. I was just a first-year student at the time. The vice-chancellor said, "I wish I had been alive in the days of Gautama Buddha. I would have gone to his feet."

I interfered and I said, "Please reconsider this. Please think it over once again and then speak. Really, would you have gone to Buddha's feet? In this life, have you gone to the feet of any beggar? Buddha was a beggar. Have you gone to the feet of any beggar who is a teacher, a teacher of the invisible world? As far as I know, you have never gone to any. So please reconsider whether, had you been alive in Buddha's day, you would have gone to his feet, whether you would have recognized him. Have you recognized anyone in this life?"

He was bewildered; he was taken aback. He became silent. He said, "I take my words back, because I never thought it over before. Really, I have never gone to anyone, so it seems logical that I would not have gone to Buddha. And even if I had passed by him, I would not have looked at him, I would not have recognized him."

It is not so that whoever came in contact with Buddha recognized him. It is not so! Sometimes Buddha passed through a village and no one recognized him. His own father did not recognize him. Even with his own wife there was no recognition.

I am here. You cannot recognize what is inside; only the outside is known. You become acquainted with only the outside, but that is how it has to be. You are not in contact with your own innerness, so how can you be in contact with mine? That is an impossibility.

But it becomes easy if you are in contact with your own innerness. Then you can be in contact with my innerness, or innerness as such. Otherwise you will just go on asking me questions and I will continue answering you. Then everything just misses the point.

I answer you not in order that you should get the answer from my answer. No, I never hope against hope, I never hope that my answer can become your answer. I know very well that my answer is of no use to you. Then why do I go on answering your questions? I go on answering, not in order that my answer will become your answer, but because, if you can listen to me silently, totally, in that silent listening you will come directly upon your own innerness. Suddenly it can explode in you; suddenly you can be in another world that is completely different from any world in which you have been living.

And if that happens, then you have come into a new existence. That new existence is your own. It is an esoteric, inner secret. That inner existence has everything you are asking.

Appendix
Awakening: A Group Work

Awakening is possible even in a single moment. In a single moment, one can explode into the divine. It is possible, but generally it never happens. One has to struggle continuously for many lives, because the task is arduous.

One cannot awaken himself. It is like this: if one is sleeping in the morning, there is every possibility that he can dream he is awake. But he will not be awake; it will just be a dream.

If a group of people decide collectively to make some effort to awaken, then it is more possible that sleep can be broken. So awakening is really a group work. It can happen individually—and each individual is capable of awakening on his own—but ordinarily it never happens that way because we never work to our utmost capacity. We never use more than ten percent of our posibilities. Ninety percent remains just potential; it is never used. Whether you are asleep or awake, there is no difference in your dreaming. Dreaming continues inside you. The awakening, the awareness that we all have, is only superficial. Deep inside, there is a dream that continues.

There are two possibilities: either individual work is possible or group work is needed. The order of *sannyas* was created to help group work to happen. If there are ten thousand people working in a group, awakening becomes more possible. Then if even one is awakened, he can create a chain of awakenings around him.

Buddha created a group order; Mahavir created a group order. Their orders were an outward phenomenon. They were orders of *sannyasins*. Inwardly, the *sannyasins* were working as a group and the group work that they were doing may have continued for many lives. For example, there are still persons alive who were part of Buddha's group of *sannysins*.

There is an inner understanding and an inner oath taken by those in the group: a promise to the group that whenever one is awakened he will do his utmost to awaken others—particularly those belonging to the group. Why particularly those belonging to the group? Because every school has a particular technique. If you have worked with a particular technique in your previous lives, you can easily work with it in this life.

For example, there are many people who have been working with me in other births, in other lives. This group of people is more capable than others in many ways. They have worked in certain ways, they have done certain things. They have progressed up to a point. It is not just a beginning for them.

With every new person who comes, I have to do much un-necessary and unessential work. For example, intellectual work is needed for beginners, but those who have worked with a particu-lar technique in their past lives will not need to do any intellectual work now. You tell them the technique and they just begin to do it. There is no need for intellectual work; they will not ask superfi-cial questions. That curiosity will not be there.

That curiosity takes much time and much energy, so one can work with beginners if one has many more lives ahead; but if one has no other life ahead, he cannot work with beginners. He has to confine his work to the old ones who are somehow on the bank. They do not need any intellectual philosophy. They have no superficial inquiries; they will go deep, directly.

The old requirement—the requirement that one should have faith—is really a trick. It is just to distinguish between the old ones and the new ones. With the new ones, faith is impossible.

Only doubt is possible. Only with the old ones is faith possible. With them, doubt is impossible.

So faith is just a technique, a trick, to choose between the old and the new, and to know on whom more work can be done in less time. It is not that those who can have faith are in any way different from those who have doubts. It is only that those who have faith have worked before somewhere, so intellectual curiosity is not there. It has been fulfilled. They have passed through it. They are not just entering the school; they have gone past the entrance. So to ask for faith is to ask, "Have you worked in your past lives?" Only if you have worked before can you have faith, otherwise not.

In today's world, doubt seems much more prominent, much easier. Faith is very difficult. The reason is not that the human mind has changed, the reason is only this: the old traditions are running thin. Really, since Nanak there have been no new traditions. Now all the religions are old. They have been going on and on; the river grows more narrow every day.

With every day that passes, there are fewer persons who belong to each tradition. Twenty-five centuries have now passed since Buddha. The tradition is so old that almost all of those who were connected with the living Master are already liberated. And all those who have remained behind, who have not yet reached, are just third rate. They have had centuries of continuous work and still they have not reached!

All the traditions are, in a way, so old now. That is why there is less faith. In the past there were so many living traditions and so many persons who had worked in their past lives. Faith was deeply rooted in each. Doubt was very difficult.

So if you ask me what I am doing, I am doing many things. One is working for those who have been connected with me in the past in any way. And there are many of them. Another is to create a new continuity that can be lived in the coming days. No old way of thinking is of any use now.

But still, I do not want to divert anyone from a path that he has been on continuously for many lives. It is useless to change his path now. It is better to let him go deep within his own tradition—not to change him, but to make his tradition alive again. Then he can go deeply within it and he will create a link with the old.

Previously I was working with new seekers so my emphasis was on doubt. I will always be concerned with doubt because only through doubt can you attract new seekers, never through faith. Faith attracts the old ones who have been doing something in their past lives. My emphasis has been on doubt because I am working for the creation of a new tradition that will be living, alive.

But now my emphasis will be on faith. And there is no contradiction in it. I am only changing the point of entrance, nothing else. When I was emphasizing doubt, no one came. Now I will emphasize faith. I will work for those with whom I was connected in past lives. Then there will be no difficulty.

When I say "doubt," when I say "faith," it looks inconsistent. Only the labeling is different. Different words will come now, but whatever I was doing before will continue. Only now, my emphasis will be on those who have already worked in the past.

That is why I have created a new order of *sannyas* now. With doubt, it could not be created. When there is doubt, one can be alone but one can never work in a group. Doubt makes you an island, but when you become a continent, you are joined with others. Then there is no separation between you and others, and you can work within a group.

As far as man is concerned, he is so weak that he cannot be relied upon individually. By himself he cannot do anything; he can only deceive himself. So if one is going to work on individuals, mechanical devices will have to be created.

For example, if you are asleep and there is no one to awaken you, you will have to use an alarm clock. It is a mechanical device that is there to help you. But no mechanical device will be very helpful for long because you will become used to it. Soon your sleep will not be disturbed by the alarm clock. Rather, it can become even more sound. The working of the mind is such that you can incorporate the sound of the alarm into your dream. Then it will not disturb your sleep. The alarm will just become a part of your dream so it will not awaken you. Sleep will continue.

I have tried working individually with many persons. I have given them mechanical devices, but they have become accustomed to them. And then a new fallacy arises, the greatest fallacy that can happen in spirituality. One can dream that he is awake! That is the most fatal disease, the most dangerous. You can continue your sleep and you can dream you are awake. Then there is no need for devices. You are left alone in your dreams.

So my emphasis from now on will be on group work. Even if someone awakens for just a single moment, he can create a shock for others. He can shake them, awaken them. So my new order of *sannyas* will be a group working with inner faith. When you feel, even for a single second, that awareness is coming to you, help others. And when the need is there, they will help you.*

---

*Although there are Rajneesh centers all over the world, Shree Rajneesh Ashram in Poona, India, is the main center around which the group work Bhagwan Shree has spoken about is taking place. There, Bhagwan Shree is guiding each of his disciples (as well as visitors from abroad) in the techniques and tradition to which each belongs. There, too, the groundwork is being laid for a new tradition that is rapidly evolving around Bhagwan Shree. In addition to the monthly meditation camps (from the eleventh to the twentieth of each month), the daily lectures, and the daily *darshans* in which small groups of seekers meet with Bhagwan Shree for individual guidance, the ashram also offers groups in primal therapy, encounter techniques, enlightenment intensives, hypnotherapy, marathons, African dancing, t'ai chi, vipassana, yoga, karate-do, massage, and other disciplines and games. For further information, contact Shree Rajneesh Ashram, 17 Koregaon Park, Poona, India.

Rajneesh Meditation Centers

MAIN CENTER

Shree Rajneesh Ashram, 17 Koregaon Park, Poona 411 001, India. Tel.: 28127. (There are dozens of centers throughout India.)

UNITED STATES AND CANADA

Ananda: 29 East 28th Street, New York, N.Y. 10016. Tel.: 212–686–3261.

Anand Taru: 25 Harbell St., Lexington, Mass. 02173

Arvind: 1330 Renfrew Street, Vancouver, B.C., Canada.

Bodhitaru: 7231 S.W. 62d Place, Miami, Fla. 33143

Devalayam: P.O. Box 592, Kansas City, Missouri 64141. Tel.: 816–753–2331.

Devagar: 310 Petit Brule, Ste. Madeleine de Rigaud, P.Q. JOP IPD, Canada. Tel.: 514–451–5565.

Dhyanataru: c/o Wyatt, Box 143, N. Berwick, Maine 03906.

Geetam: Box 576, Highway 18, Lucerne Valley, Calif. 92356. Tel.: 714–248–6163.

Madhuban: 10 Winslow St., Provincetown, Mass. 02657. Tel.: 617–487–0669.

Neelamber: Blackmore Lane, P.O. Box 143, East Islip, N.Y. 11730. Tel.: 516–581–0004.

Paras: P.O. Box 22174, San Francisco, Calif. 94122. Tel.: 415–664–6600.

Satsang: 887 North La Salle, Chicago, Ill. 60610 Tel.: 312-943-8561/8549.

Sarvam: 6412 Luzon Ave., Washington, D.C. 20012.

EUROPE

Amitabh: Korte Prinsengracht 9/II, Amsterdam, Holland. Tel.: 238-966.

Anand Lok: 1 Berlin 61, Mehringdamm 61, West Germany. Postal Address: 1 Berlin 61, Luckenwalderstrasse 11, West Germany.

Anand Niketan: Kobmagergade 43, 1150, Copenhagen K, Denmark.

Arihant: Via Cacciatori della Alli 19, 20019 Settimo Milanese, Milano, Italy.

Gourishankar: 9 Ravensdean Gardens, Penicuik, Midlothian, Scotland. Tel.: Penicuik 73034.

Kalptaru: Top floor, 10a Belmont Street, London NW1, England. Tel.: 01-267-8304. Postal address: 28 Oak Village, London NW5 4QN, England.

Nirvana: 82 Bell Street, London NW1, England. Tel.: 01-262-0991.

Prasthan: 21 Wilmot Road, Glasgow C13 1XL, Scotland.

Prempatti: 45-390 Desmonts, France.

Premtaru: Church Farm House, Field Dalling, Holt, Norfolk, England.

Purvodaya: D-8051 Margaretenried, Fongí-Hof, West Germany.

Satyam: 15 b route de Loex, 1213 Onex, Switzerland. Tel.: 93-19-46.

Shantidweep: 25 Avenue Pierre, Premier de Serbie, Paris XVIe, France. Tel.: 721-7930.

Shreyas: 8 Munich 60, Raucheneggerstrasse 4/II, West Germany. Tel.: 089-882-662.

Suryodaya: The Old Rectory, Gislingham by Diss, Nr Eye, Suffolk, England.

Trimurt: 1 Ruedes Templiers, Grimaud, France 83360. Tel.: 432108.

Tushita: North Moreton, Didcot, Oxfordshire 119BA, England.

ELSEWHERE

Anand Need: P.O. Box 72424, Nairobi, Kenya, East Africa.
Asheesh: c/o Oda, Kanagawa-Ken, Chigasaki-She, Tomoe 2–8–23, Japan.
Purnam: Caixa Postale 1966, Porto Alegre—Rio G. do Sul, Brazil. Tel.: 21888.
Shanti Niketan: 10 Bayfield Road, Herne Bay, Auckland, New Zealand.
Shanti Shila: 56 Dona Magdalena Hemady St., Quezon City, Philippines.
Soma: Rua Caraibas 1179, Casa 9, 05020 Pompeia, Sao Paulo, Brazil.